Publication #12 in the "On Target"
Series of Outdoor Sports Publications
from Glenn Helgeland's
TARGET COMMUNICATIONS

1st Printing 6/95

MUZZLELOADING FOR WHITETAILS
AND OTHER BIG GAME

by Toby Bridges

Library of Congress Number: 94-49359

TARGET COMMUNICATIONS CORPORATION
7626 W. Donges Bay Rd.
Mequon, WI 53097

ISBN: 0-913305-12-X

Library of Congress Cataloging-in-Publication Data

Bridges, Toby.
   Muzzleloading for whitetails and other big game / by Toby Bridges. p. cm. — (Publication number 12 in the "On Target" series of outdoor sports publications)

   1. Muzzleloader hunting. 2. White-tailed deer hunting.
   I. Title. II. Series: "On Target" series :publication no. 12.
SK39.2.B75   1995   799.2'13—dc20   94-49359
ISBN 0-913305-12-X (pbk.)   CIP

Copyright ©1995 by Target Communications Corporation. All rights reserved

No part of this book may be reproduced in any form or by any means, except for the inclusion of brief quotations in a review, without permission in writing from the publisher. Printed in the United States of America by Ripon Community Printers, Ripon, Wisconsin.

Cover photos by Toby Bridges

CONTENTS

Introduction. 1

Chapter 1
Introduction to Muzzleloading. 9

Chapter 2
Hunting the Third Season 25

Chapter 3
Muzzleloading Enters A New Era. 35

Chapter 4
Selecting a Muzzleloading Rifle 45

Chapter 5
Accessories or Necessities? 55

Chapter 6
Working Up Hunting Loads 63

Chapter 7
Sighting In & Making the Shot 75

Chapter 8
Ten Steps to Better Muzzleloading Rifle Accuracy 85

Chapter 9
Muzzleloaders Must Be Cleaned 95

Chapter 10
Hunting the Early Seasons 103

Chapter 11
Hunting the Late Seasons 111

Chapter 12
The Muzzleloading Alternative. 123

Chapter 13
Muzzleloading for Other Big Game 131

Chapter 14
The Future of Hunting With a Muzzleloader 143

The Author

Toby Bridges began hunting whitetails in his home state of Illinois at the age of 13. This Midwestern state is one of many which have required the use of modern shotguns loaded with rifled or saboted slugs for whitetails, or as an option a hunter could carry a rifle of frontloading design. After a single season of hunting deer with his father's favorite old Winchester Model 12 "quail gun", Toby decided to try his hand at hunting deer with a more accurate muzzleloading rifle.

He purchased his first frontloader at the age of 14 and used it for whitetails that second season afield, in both his home state and in neighboring Missouri. Those hunts helped set the stage for a lifetime of black powder hunting. In each, Toby took eight-point bucks with his first muzzleloader, a .45 caliber Dixie Gun Works "Kentucky" rifle.

Since that first successful muzzleloading season, Toby has tagged another 80 muzzleloader whitetails, 12 of which qualify for The Longhunter Society record book of muzzleloader-harvested big game. His experience with muzzleloaders has also allowed him to take more than a hundred other big game animals with a frontloading rifle.

During his 30+ years of hunting with a muzzleloader, he has written more than 800 magazine articles and four books on muzzleloading. A majority of his articles have centered on hunting the whitetail deer with frontloading black powder rifles, his favorite pastime. He has also produced a one-hour video on hunting whitetails with a muzzleloader and included several hunts on another one-hour video production. Toby also has appeared on several nationally distributed television shows, talking about hunting with a muzzleloader.

He has been closely involved with the muzzleloading industry more than 20 years. In addition to promoting the sport through his articles and books, he has worked closely with the developers of numerous muzzleloading products and guns. Several of today's better selling muzzleloading rifles are of his design, and he was actively involved in the refinement of the now popular in-line percussion ignition rifles. Likewise, he also did much to popularize the use of the effective saboted handgun bullets for deer and other big game.

Muzzleloading has gone through major changes in the past 30 years, and Toby Bridges has been a big influence on the maturity of muzzleloading into a true hunting sport.

Introduction

A New "Old Way" To Hunt Whitetails

Pardon my English, but muzzleloading just ain't the same ol' sport! Since the rebirth of muzzleloading during the late 1950s and early 1960s, the sport has made a 180 degree turn. Back then, nostalgia was the big reason for black powder shooting....do it the way the pioneers did. Today, nostalgia plays a lesser and lesser role in the reasons a person picks up a muzzleloader. Today's black powder shooter is a hunter, and he wants the most effective rifle and load he can carry into the deer woods.

Muzzleloading doesn't have to be old-fashioned if today's hunter doesn't want it to be; on the other hand, it still can be if he wants it to be. Within the limitations of black powder ballistics, some of today's modern in-line percussion ignition rifle designs are capable of delivering centerfire rifle-quality accuracy at 100 yards, and farther! To make these rifles even more effective on whitetails and other big game, jacketed hollow-point pistol bullets are quickly replacing the old soft lead round balls and heavy conical bullets.

Depending upon which expert you ask, there are an estimated 2-1/2 million to 3-1/2 million black powder hunters from coast to coast, and the number continues to grow at an unbelievable rate. Muzzleloading is recognized as the fastest growing of today's shooting and hunting sports in attracting new participants on an annual basis. The reason for this explosive growth is simple — muzzleloading seasons across the country offer some of the best hunting opportunities.

Trying to determine which came first, muzzleloading guns which attracted new black powder shooters or new black powder shooters who demanded a better variety of frontloading rifles is in the chicken-or-egg category. The fact remains that the current crop of modern muzzleloading rifles is the best we have ever had, catering more and more to the hunter's needs and preferences.

Many of today's frontloaders are capable of printing a hollow-point bullet group inside 1-1/2 inches at 100 yards. Performance such as this was unheard of 20 years ago!

Muzzleloading whitetail seasons will continue to attract converts from the ranks of centerfire firearm and archery hunters. **A look at the creation of new hunting opportunities over the past couple of decades reveals that the vast majority have been the establishment or expansion of muzzleloading seasons.** Record numbers of hunters have added the sport of muzzleloading to their fall activities to expand their time in the field.

The establishment of The Longhunter Society record book of muzzleloading big game, administered by the National Muzzle Loading Rifle Association, also has created new interest in hunting with a muzzleloader. It is a trophy hunter's best shot at getting into the record books.

Here, finally, is an up-to-date book on hunting with a muzzleloading rifle, written for the serious as well as the beginning black powder hunter. In the following pages, we will cover the latest guns and loads, plus many of the old favorites.

That was then. . . .

• *The author decked out in all his mountain man finery. It was the thing to do back then, when the black powder movement first began and was filled with nostalgia.*

• *Rendezvous were big then. Authenticity was a motivating force....along with swapping stuff, "yarning" stories around the campfire and such. Photo by Tom Fegely.*

THIS is now....

The author with a record-book whitetail he took on a late season Minnesota hunt. Photo by Tom Fegely.

And THIS is now....

Photo by Richard P. Smith.

With today's muzzleloaders, you CAN get benchrest accuracy at 100 to 150 yards .... much greater distances than previously were possible.

And THIS is now....

Photo by Tom Fegely

Photo by Gary Clancy

● *Serious deer hunters with serious muzzleloading equipment ... hunting deer in early season, regular season and late season ... using every technique known in fields, in tree stands, on the ground, on the water.*

Photo by Richard P. Smith

Photo by Richard P. Smith

And THIS is now....

Photo by Gary Clancy

WOMEN **YOUTH**

HERD MANAGEMENT **TROPHY HUNTING**

Photo by Richard P. Smith *Photo by Richard P. Smith*

And THIS is now....

Photo by Tom Fegely

Photo by Betty Lou Fegely

DEER
DEER
DEER

Photo by Richard P. Smith

Chapter 1
Introduction to Muzzleloading

Muzzleloaders in their simplest form came to the Americas with the first settlers who sailed across the Atlantic from Europe. Columbus' expedition carried crude matchlock military-style muskets, as did following expeditions and, later, the Pilgrims. While most refinements of the firearm ignition system took place in Europe, many were prompted by the necessity of a more reliable muzzleloading ignition system in the "New World". The necessity was not only for protection, but also for putting meat on the table.

With the early settlers came talented gun makers, from Germany, France and England. By the mid-1700s, some of the world's finest riflesmiths were found on this side of the Atlantic Ocean, building muzzleloaders which better fit the needs of the adventurers who settled the untamed lands, or who explored the vast wilderness which lay even farther to the west and north. The needs of the "longhunter" shaped the development of the long and slender Kentucky rifle and later the shorter, faster-handling half-stock rifles which helped tame the country west of the Mississippi. A study of changes in muzzleloader design in this country is a study of American history itself.

Yet, as old as muzzleloading is, it's still a whole new world for today's hunter looking to try his hand at taking a whitetail or any other big game animal with a slow-to-load firearm of frontloading design. The hunter looking to make the best possible decision could be more than just a little intimidated by all the choices now available, especially if he knows little, if anything, about what makes a muzzleloader an effective big game rifle. This book has been written to eliminate beginning fears and to help even those of you who are experienced black powder hunters make your muzzleloading hunts more successful and enjoyable.

The biggest mistake most beginning black powder hunters make is to choose a muzzleloader strictly on appearance....it looks neat. They get hung up on styling without considering how the rifle will perform in the field.

If you're a serious hunter getting into muzzleloading more for the opportunity to hunt than to relive a bit of history, you MUST first consider several hunting related questions.

1) What is the most effective projectile for hunting deer and other big game?

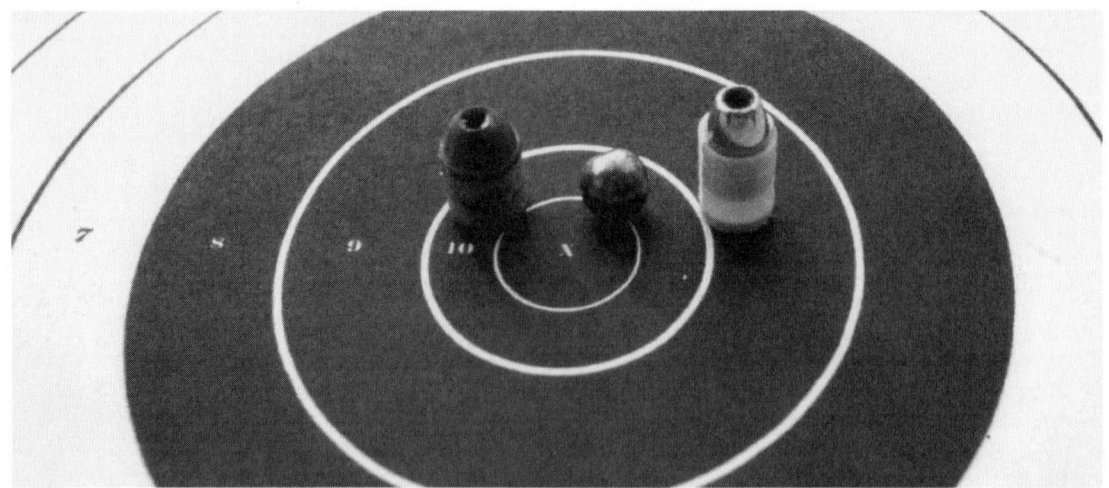
• *Before deciding on a particular style of rifle to buy, first determine the projectile you want to hunt with — round ball or conical. Shown here, left to right, are conical, round ball and saboted conical. Photo by Gary Clancy.*

When purchasing a muzzleloader solely for hunting, this should be your first question. In addition, in several regions of the country state regulations will dictate which projectile(s) you can and cannot hunt with. A third factor is personal preference; you may not want the most effective projectile, preferring, instead, to go with nostalgia. After you have faced these concerns, then look for the rifle which will allow you to shoot the style of projectile you have decided upon.

It takes an entirely different rifle to get the absolute best performance from a patched round ball than from a conical hunting bullet, and vice versa. A round ball rifle features a slow rate of rifling twist, allowing the patch to grip the grooves of the rifling and transfer the spin of the rifling to the soft lead ball. If the rifling spins too fast, the ball can resist being spun by the patch and accuracy is usually pretty lousy.

On the other hand, when you're selecting a rifle to shoot a heavy conical or even a modern saboted pistol bullet, concentrate on those models which feature a much faster rate of rifling twist. Conical bullets are often twice as long as they are in diameter, sometimes more than twice as long. Being longer, the bullets require a considerable amount of gyroscopic spin to stabilize them in flight. A much faster rifling twist is needed to impart that spin to the bullet.

There is no such thing as a rate of rifling twist which will let you shoot the patched round ball and the heavier conical bullet equally as accurate. If a rifle has been designed to shoot a certain type of projectile, all the work in the world won't make it perform with a different projectile design. To help you make a wiser selection of the rifle you will be carrying for whitetails, turn to the chapter of this book on "Selecting A Muzzleloading Deer Rifle".

2) What is the best caliber to use for deer?

For the modern centerfire rifle hunter just looking to get into muzzleloading, a bore as big as .45 seems awfully large. Most modern rifle hunters have become accustomed to shooting rifles of .243, .270, .30/30 and .30/06 calibers. To move up to something as large as a .35 Remington, .35 Whelen, or even a .338 is to go after whitetails with a cannon.

However, with a muzzleloader, you must learn to cope with the slower ballistics and limited range of black powder loads. Those loads aren't producing the high velocities of most popular centerfire calibers and likewise aren't getting the extreme shock that a 130- to 150-grain bullet delivers when it hits at nearly 3,000 feet per second (fps). The effectiveness of a muzzleloader is a combination of retained energy and the diameter of the projectile that makes the entrance wound. Then, of course, there is the

- Most early muzzleloaders built in America displayed strong European influence. This copy of a late German flintlock "jaeger" was custom built by the author.

- An in-line percussion frontloader with stainless steel barrel and thumbhole stock is a state-of-the-art black powder hunting rifle.

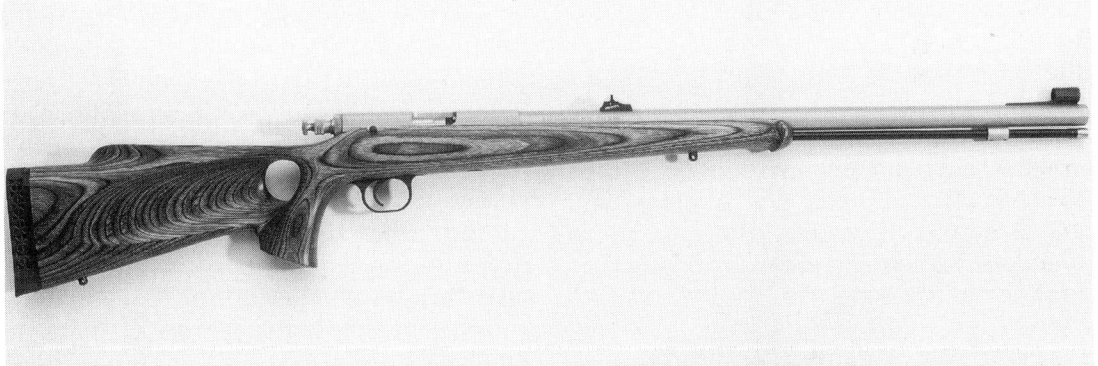

performance of the projectile itself once it's inside the animal, expanding and transferring energy to the target. When a bullet starts out at .45, .50 or .54 caliber, then begins to flatten out and expand into .60 or .80 caliber, it can deliver quite a wallop.

Even so, bigger is not always better. Most knowledgeable muzzleloading hunters have established the .50 caliber bore as the optimum bore size for big game hunting. Turn to the chapter on "Working Up Hunting Loads" and you'll learn what performance to expect from the different calibers with a variety of bullets. The chapter also details powder charges needed to develop adequate energy levels.

3) What is the maximum effective range of a muzzleloading hunting rifle?

For years, many black powder "experts" led us to believe that the absolute maximum effective range of any muzzleloading big game rifle was a hundred yards, no matter what projectile was loaded. At the same time, these same "experts" occasionally would tout the long range killing power of the old Sharps and other single-shot breechloading black powder cartridge rifles of the late 1800s. I ask you: If those rifles could cleanly take big game out to 200 yards shooting a 300- to 400-grain bullet ahead of 100 grains of black powder, why won't a muzzleloader?

Truth is, a muzzleloader stuffed with the right powder charge and bullet combination is fully capable of taking game at distances nearly double the old 100 yard maximum once preached. What today's black powder hunter has to cope with is the poor trajectory once the shot is out past 150 yards. "Sighting In and Making the Shot" is the

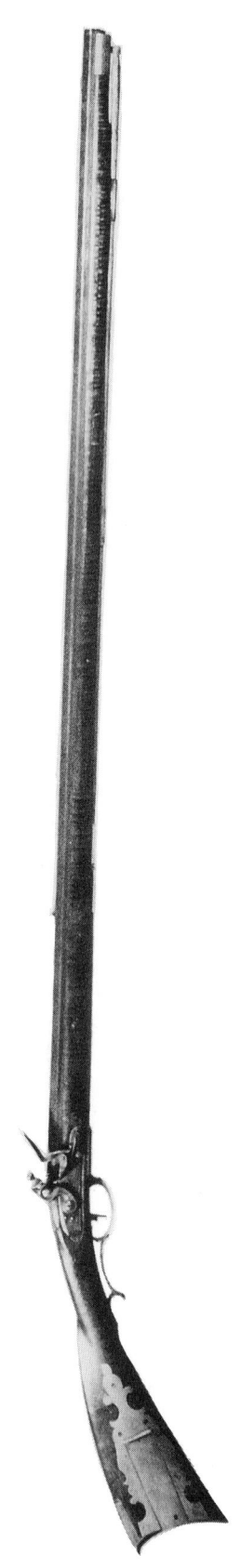

• The long barrels of the famed Pennsylvania and Kentucky longrifles were an American trademark.

chapter of this book which will give pointers on sighting in a muzzleloading rifle to take best advantage of the trajectory you'll have to learn to live with.

In a number of states, either statewide or in designated zones which can make up much of the state, the modern centerfire firearm deer hunter is faced with going after whitetails with a modern shotgun loaded with rifled or saboted shotgun slugs. In all those states, muzzleloading hunting rifles can be carried as an option. And, thanks to the performance of some of today's efficient and accurate modern in-line percussion models loaded with a saboted handgun bullet, these rifles can actually give the black powder deer hunter an advantage. Turn to the chapter "The Muzzleloading Alternative' and learn why.

These three are just some of the questions anyone new to muzzleloading often asks before buying a muzzleloader. The hunter who seeks answers from someone who is really knowledgeable about muzzleloading is sure to make a better choice when he or she parts with hard-earned cash to buy a frontloading deer rifle.

One bit of caution, however: **Don't take the advice of just one person you think knows a lot about muzzleloading.** There are lots of shooters who know a lot about a small segment of the sport and the guns available. Their enthusiasm for a certain design or style of rifle could steer you away from a rifle which would be much better suited for your needs....and your preferences, once you determine them.

The information contained in this book represents more than 30 years of muzzleloading experience and, I believe, does more to cover the sport of black powder hunting than any other book in print today. If you haven't already bought a muzzleloading whitetail rifle, let this book be your guide to making the right choice. If you already have acquired a rifle, this book will help you learn how to obtain the best performance from your frontloader.

Believe me, once you have bought that black powder rifle, it doesn't mean that suddenly you've learned everything you need to know. In fact, most shooters suddenly

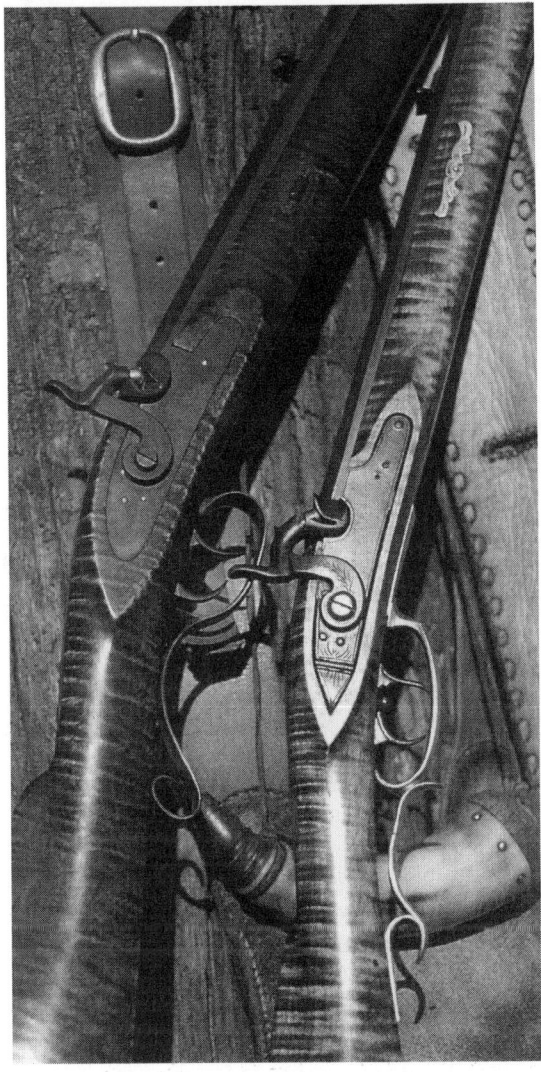

• *Traditional rifles of authentic styling are available for those who demand such qualities in their frontloader. However, today's emphasis is more on performance on big game.*

realize they have a lot more questions which need answering before they feel comfortable with loading and shooting a type of firearm with which they have little or no experience. Let's take a look at the more common questions and concerns.

What accessories or loading aids are needed to load and shoot a muzzleloading hunting rifle?

Muzzleloading is a sport which has been plagued by an unbelievable assortment of gadgets and goodies. Unfortunately, most of these generally don't amount to much more than gimmicks which work better in theory than in practical application. Sorting the "necessities" from the gadgetry can be a nightmare for the inexperienced shooter.

In the chapter "Accessories or Necessities?" we take a look at what really is needed to load and shoot any muzzleloading deer rifle. You will be surprised how simple things can be kept and still get top performance from a muzzleloader. In fact, keeping things simple often is the key to being successful when hunting whitetails with a black powder rifle.

If a new muzzleloading rifle just won't shoot as well as advertised, or as expected, what can I do to improve performance?

Great performance from a muzzleloading rifle begins with making the right selection. If the loads you shoot simply aren't accurate, be sure you're shooting the projectile for which the rifle was designed. Remember, a patched round ball most of the time won't produce acceptable accuracy out of a rifle with a fast rate of rifling twist. Likewise, a long conical bullet generally won't give acceptable accuracy out of a barrel with a slow rate of rifling twist.

Even if you are shooting the right projectile for the rifle purchased, don't expect much in return unless you bought a quality muzzleloader. Just because a frontloader is built with a rifled bore doesn't mean it's going to shoot accurately. Some rifling processes don't produce the best rifling, and poor or rough rifling can render a muzzleloader useless.

If the muzzleloader is of shoddy quality to start with, there probably isn't much hope for it. However, if you've spent the money to purchase a rifle of acceptable to top quality and still can't get it to perform

• *Some bench rest shooting is necessary to determine how well your rifle is shooting and, if there are problems, help you through your troubleshooting checklist. Photo by Gary Clancy.*

up to your expectations, there could be a simple reason. Often, it boils down to operator error in loading the rifle. However, it also could be a slight problem with the rifle itself. The chapter "Ten Steps to Better Muzzleloading Rifle Accuracy" can help diagnose what ails a problem muzzleloader and simplify troubleshooting.

How often must a muzzleloader be cleaned?

This is the number one concern of most hunters looking to switch from a relatively clean, smokeless powder centerfire rifle to a dirty, smelly black powder rifle. Well, if you shoot a muzzleloader, you have to clean that muzzleloader. This is a commitment you make when you decide to take up black powder shooting. It comes with the territory.

Both black powder and the substitute powder known as Pyrodex are totally water soluble, so a dirty muzzleloader can be cleaned easily without anything else. Water often was all the early pioneers and explorers had to clean their rifles and, far from civilization, they knew the importance of keeping their frontloaders clean and in serviceable condition.

Many of today's newer models are much more user friendly than the original guns of the late 1700s and 1800s. For one thing, they break down for easier cleaning than do guns of more traditional design. Some even allow the breech plug to be completely removed for a thorough cleaning from the breech end. By being able to look all the way through the bore, there's no doubt in your mind whether the rifle is clean.

While many of today's rifles are easier to clean and care for, there still aren't any shortcuts to cleaning a muzzleloader once it has been fired. In recent years, several manufacturers have introduced and marketed miracle lubes which they claim eliminate the need to thoroughly scrub a bore at the end of a day's shooting. Don't you believe it!! Even if your rifle is one of the newer stainless steel models, be advised that to put off cleaning for only a day or two following a shooting session could ruin the rifle's bore.

Keeping a muzzleloader clean takes some effort, but it doesn't have to be a chore. In the chapter "Muzzleloaders Must Be Cleaned" this book covers the best methods for cleaning various muzzleloading rifle designs, cleaning solvents which can make the job less tedious in deer camp, and the cleaning accessories which simplify the task.

If I enjoy hunting whitetails with a muzzleloader, can I use the same rifle to hunt elk and other big game?

My favorite .50 caliber muzzleloading whitetail rifle has been used to take a number of North American big game species. I've used the rifle on elk, moose, caribou, black bear, pronghorn and mule deer. The key to using a muzzleloading whitetail rifle on other big game species is to match the load with the game being hunted. It takes a lot more punch to bring down a moose or elk than it does a pronghorn antelope. Once again, this all boils down to being able to shoot the right projectile for the job, which in turn means selecting the most versatile hunting frontloader you can buy.

Muzzleloading is just now maturing into a true hunting sport. The special muzzleloading whitetail seasons which were first established in several eastern and midwestern states paved the way for other states to follow. With this rapidly expanding interest in hunting whitetails with a frontloading rifle, it was only natural that western states followed with special black powder seasons for mule deer, elk, pronghorn, and in some states there is now even a muzzleloader-only moose hunt.

While there currently aren't many, if any, special muzzleloader hunts for bighorn sheep, mountain goats or caribou, more and more hunters are taking their muzzleloaders

• *William "Tony" Knight with a Midwestern whitetail taken with one of the modern in-line percussion rifles he designed.*

after these game animals as well. In Arizona, where fewer than 100 desert bighorn permits are issued annually, nearly 10 percent of the hunters drawn for this once-in-a-lifetime hunting opportunity are doing it with a muzzleloader, even though they could use a flat-shooting 7mm Remington Magnum or a .300 Winchester Magnum.

Why? Challenge has to be the number one reason. There is more satisfaction in taking a good ram with a single-shot, short range frontloading rifle than with a long range centerfire. Filling your tag with a muzzleloader means you've done it "up close and personal". Another reason is a new muzzleloading big game record book which gives trophy black powder hunters something to shoot for. (Pun fully intended.)

If you are looking to get into muzzleloading for more than just hunting whitetails, or if you are already hunting deer with a muzzleloader and would like now to carry the rifle for other big game, turn to the chapters "Muzzleloading For Other Big Game" and "Going For The Record". The first shares with you what to shoot for bigger game; the other chapter lets you know what to shoot for.

With all the advances in today's deadly accurate centerfire rifles and ammunition, why would anyone really serious about hunting even fool with a slow-to-load, single-shot and ballistically inferior muzzleloading rifle?

The fact that you are reading this book means either that you are seriously thinking about getting into muzzleloading or you already are a muzzleloading hunter. You probably already have figured out the answer to this question, or have gotten into muzzleloader hunting for purely personal reasons. As a muzzleloading hunter, however, you will surely be asked this question by some of your modern firearm hunting counterparts who still look down on muzzleloading. It was included here more for their benefit than yours.

When it comes to actual percentage

● *Outdoor writer Jim Shockey is a prime example of today's black powder hunter who is looking for an effective muzzleloader to use on all North American big game.*

● *With all the advances in today's centerfire rifles and ammunition, why would anyone seriously fool with a muzzleloader? Because it's challenging and fun and allows you to spend more hunting time afield....which is what it's all about. Photo by Richard P. Smith.*

of new growth year to year, muzzleloading continues to be the fastest growing of today's shooting sports. Sales of archery equipment still outdistance annual muzzleloader sales by at least one third, but muzzleloading is catching up. However, when it comes to new hunters making the switch -- or simply expanding their hunting time with another shooting tool -- there's no denying that the highest percentage of growth goes to muzzleloading. As this was written, several states already have broken the barrier of 100,000 issued muzzleloader permits, and a few others are quickly closing in. A growing number of states also now issue more muzzleloader deer permits than archery tags.

The simple reason: hunting with a muzzleloader is fun, a lot of fun. However, the real reason for the growing popularity of hunting with a frontloading rifle goes deeper than that. It boils down to new hunting opportunities.

Deer herds, principally whitetail herds, continue to grow all across the country. Unlike 20 to 25 years ago when deer populations were considerably lower in nearly all states, today's game managers are more concerned about under-harvesting the whitetail. In many parts of the country there are now simply too many deer for available cover, forage or habitat. Game departments are now relying on muzzleloading as another effective management tool to increase harvest numbers. This means increased hunting opportunities for today's whitetail hunter looking to extend his hunting season .... or seasons.

There also are those pessimists among us who feel that in the not so distant future we will see so many restrictions imposed on owning a modern cartridge firearm that most hunters won't want to bother. Some are biting the bullet now and getting into muzzleloading to build more experience with the frontloaders; they feel these will be the last rifles we will be allowed to hunt with.

I'm more optimistic than that. While I do feel that we will see more restrictions placed on owning a modern firearm, I don't think this country will ever get to the point where American citizens are refused the right to own a firearm. In this country, firearms are our heritage. Without them, we would not enjoy the freedoms we do today.

However, I'm also a realist. As population levels continue to grow, especially surrounding metropolitan areas, I feel we will see greater restrictions on the types of firearms allowed when hunting whitetails. Once there is a house on every 20- to 40-acre woodlot, the use of centerfire rifles is sure to be curtailed. In some 20 states, their use has already been curtailed,

• *Greg Bambenek with a Kentucky buck he rattled in. Photo by Richard P. Smith.*

either statewide or in zones which make up as much as 50 percent to 60 percent of the state. In these areas, regulations call for the use of shorter range shotguns loaded with rifled or saboted slugs, or in every instance the muzzleloader can be carried as an alternative.

The chapters "Hunting The Third Season" and "The Future of Hunting With a Muzzleloader" further explore why today's hunter is turning to muzzleloading.

Muzzleloading is a many-faceted sport. Within its parameters you will find shooters from all walks of life who have gotten into the sport for varied reasons. This book is for those of you who have taken to muzzleloading in order to hunt with a frontloader, for whatever reason. It is not a history book chronicling the lifestyles of early explorers or fur traders; it is not a "how to" book for the reader looking to make his own moccasins or tan his own deer skins, nor is it simply a collection of tall hunting tales. This book is for those millions of modern day muzzleloading hunters who head afield each fall and winter to fill their tags with a black powder rifle. **This is a book on hunting with a muzzleloader.**

● More and more hunters are heading into woods, fields and mountains each year, muzzleloader in hand, intent on filling their tags with a black powder rifle. Photo by Gary Clancy.

Intro to Muzzleloading

Why a glossary here?

Seems like a good idea to go through the specialized terms *before* you wade into the meat of the book rather than after. It will help with comprehension, enjoyment and usefulness.

GLOSSARY

Aperture rear sight - Often referred to as a "peep" sight since it requires the shooter visually to center the front sight in the center of the small round hole in the rear sight while aiming. This arrangement makes it one of the most accurate metallic sights.

Ball - Spherical lead projectile loaded into a muzzleloading rifle using a cloth patch. Accuracy with a round ball usually requires that the rifle feature slow-twist rifling of one-turn-in-60 to-72 inches.

Ball screw - Ramrod accessory resembling a wood screw which threads into the end of the ramrod and is used to remove a ball or bullet which has been loaded into a barrel without a powder charge, or to pull a bullet which cannot be seated all the way down on the powder charge.

Barrel - The round, octagonal, etc., metal tube through and from which the ball, bullet or buckshot emerges upon being fired.

Barrel key - A wedge-shaped flat key which holds the barrel in place with the forestock on many half-stock muzzleloading rifles.

Barrel pin - Small, round metal pin which passes through the forestock and through "tenons" on the bottom of the barrel to fasten the barrel to the long forestock of full-stocked "Kentucky" styled rifles.

Black powder - The traditional propellant used in muzzleloading guns, consisting of a mixture of potassium nitrate, charcoal and sulphur.

Bore - The drilling or hole (rifled or smoothbore) through which the projectile travels the length of the barrel.

Bore build-up - A condition where powder fouling continues to build with each additional shot. With black powder "bore build-up" can be so great with just several shots that getting the next shot loaded can be next to impossible.

Breech - As pertaining to a muzzleloader, the end of the barrel closest to the shooter, where the seated projectile and powder charge sits at the moment of ignition.

Breech Plug - The threaded plug that screws into the breech end of a muzzleloading barrel to seal that end of the barrel.

Bullet - Generally used to refer to a projectile of conical design.

Bullet mould - A set of metal blocks with a hollow cavity into which molten lead is poured to produce cast lead projectiles.

Butt plate - The plate which is fitted to the very rear of the stock and fits into the shoulder when the gun is fired. This plate can be made of metal, horn, plastic, rubber or other materials.

Caliber - Refers to the diameter of a muzzleloader's bore, commonly measured in thousandths of an inch.

Caplock - Another term often used to describe a percussion ignition system.

Corrosion - The deterioration of metal parts through chemical reaction or oxidation, the worst enemy of muzzleloading guns.

Double rifle - Side-by-side or over-and-under rifle with two barrels which offer the shooter a fast second shot.

Drop-in barrel - Commonly used to refer to

an accessory barrel which allows a black powder shooter to quickly switch his rifle from one caliber to another in a matter of seconds. Most commonly used with half-stock rifles of the "Hawken" design.

Fast-twist barrel - A term used to distinguish a barrel with rifling which spins with a fast spiral for stabilization of longer conical bullets. Fast-twist rifled barrels are those barrels with rifling which spins with a one-turn-in-20 to-32 inches.

Flintlock - An ignition system dating from the late 17th and early 18th centuries which relied on a piece of flint (held in the jaws of the hammer) striking a hardened steel surface to produce sparks for ignition. Predates the percussion ignition system.

Frizzen - The hardened steel surface which a flint strikes to produce sparks for ignition with a flintlock.

Grooves - The spiral channels cut in the bore of a rifle to produce rifling. The raised portions are referred to as lands. The lands and grooves work together to cause a bullet to rotate as it travels down the barrel and are instrumental in the frontloader's accuracy.

Group - The consistent placement of shots on the target.

Half-cock - The position of the hammer of a side-lock ignition system which positions the hammer up from and off the capped nipple or the frizzen of a flintlock. Should not be considered a safety position.

Half-stock rifle - A design which does not feature a stock which runs the full length of the barrel. While some guns may feature a forestock that runs less than half or more than half the length of the barrel, they are generally still referred to as rifles of half-stock design.

Hammer - The striker which causes the rifle to fire. A hammer can be of the side, under or in-line design.

Hang-fire - A condition when the rifle hesitates after the hammer has fallen before it actually fires. This is commonly caused in percussion guns by oil, condensation or moisture which has gotten between the percussion cap and the powder charge. With a flintlock it can be caused by a damp priming charge or by filling the flash pan too full with priming powder.

Hawken rifle - Generally used to describe a half-stock rifle of larger caliber, such as that used by the mountain men of the 1840s. Samuel and Jacob Hawken were, however, actual builders who operated most of their years out of St. Louis, Missouri. The rifles they built were for the most part heavy, large-bored, half-stock rifles which won a reputation for quality and accuracy.

Ignition - The method used to fire the main charge in the breech of a firearm, muzzleloading or breechloading.

In-line ignition - Today this commonly refers to modern-looking muzzleloaders of percussion ignition, but in the past there have even been in-line flintlock ignitions as well. The arrangement simply utilizes a plunger style hammer which causes the fire of a percussion cap (modern percussion in-line ignition) to enter the breech end of the barrel directly through the rear center of the breech plug for positive, sure-fire ignition.

Kentucky rifle - A term mistakenly used to distinguish most American built longrifles, especially those with long, slender forestocks which extend the full length of the barrel. Many so-called Kentucky longrifles were built in Pennsylvania, the Carolinas, Virginia and other early gunmaking centers.

Lapping the bore - The process of smoothing out rough areas of a rifle's bore. This is commonly done using fine abrasive compounds on a tight fitting patch or in worse cases the use of a lead plug of actual bore dimensions. Some shooters also "lap the bore" of their new rifles to slightly dull the sharp edges of freshly cut rifling.

Loading block - A loading aid which usually is a simple piece of wood with holes drilled for carrying pre-patched balls. To speed up loading, the shooter simply aligns one of the holes with the bore of the rifle and with a short starter pushes the patch and ball into the muzzle.

Lock plate - The metal plate to which the mechanical parts of a muzzleloader lock are attached.

Long rifle - The only true term that should be used to describe the style of rifle most commonly used in America during the late 1700s and into the early 1800s. The guns commonly were built with lengthy 40- to 44-inch barrels and featured a full length stock.

Mainspring - The heavy spring which produces the power for the hammer; can be of the flat "leaf" type or modern coil type.

Metallic sights - Any non-optical sight which does not rely on glass lenses and magnification, including standard open, "peep" and tube type sights.

Minie ball or bullet - An elongated projectile named after its designer Captain C.E. Minie of France and first introduced in 1848. This cylindrical bullet offered improved aerodynamics over the patched round ball. The bullet loaded easily and relied on expansion of a hollow base by the exploding powder charge for a precision fit with the rifle's (rifled musket's) bore. Designed primarily for military use, seeing widespread use during the Civil War.

Misfire - A condition when the round loaded into the barrel fails to fire, even though the percussion cap or priming powder of a flintlock may fire. A misfire can also be the result of the cap or priming powder not igniting.

Muzzle - The end opposite the breech end of the barrel, where the projectile is loaded into a "muzzleloader" and from which it is expelled.

Muzzle energy - The amount of force exerted by the projectile as it leaves the muzzle, expressed in foot-pounds.

Muzzle velocity - Speed of the projectile as it leaves the muzzle, expressed in feet per second.

Nipple - The small metal cone of a percussion muzzleloader which accepts the percussion cap for ignition. Flame from the exploding cap flows through a channel running through the nipple and into the breech end of the barrel where the main powder charge has been loaded.

Nipple wrench - A tool used specifically for removing the nipple from a percussion muzzleloader.

Patch/patching - Cloth used to form a gas-tight seal around a round ball loaded into a muzzleloader. The patch also grips the rifling of the bore and transfers the spin of the rifling to the ball for better accuracy. The cloth patch is the earliest form of a "sabot," taking up the difference in smaller diameter projectile and larger caliber bore.

Percussion cap - The small metallic cup which contains a minute amount of an explosive compound which provides ignition for percussion ignition systems. The strike of the hammer ignites the explosive compound and the resulting flash travels through the nipple to the powder charge.

Powder flask - A container for carrying or storing powder intended for use in a muzzleloading gun. Flasks have been made from a variety of materials, including brass, copper, horn, wood and antler.

Powder measure - A measuring device which allows the shooter to load a muzzleloader with consistent powder charges.

Pyrodex - Commercially available black powder substitute which duplicates the pressures, velocities and energies produced by black powder. The propellant is more readily available since it is not classified as a "Class A" explosive, which black powder is.

Ramrod - A rod used to seat the projectile over the powder charge, often made of wood, metal or synthetic materials. The ramrod is usually carried under the barrel of the muzzleloader, held in place by "ramrod thimbles" or "pipes".

Rifled musket - A rifled military musket, designed for use with the big hollow based "minie ball" or bullet. Not to be confused with a "rifle." A rifled musket has much thinner barrel walls than a rifle.

Sabot - Today made of plastic, the sabot is a loading component which allows the shooter/hunter to load a smaller diameter projectile into a larger diameter bore, i.e. a .45-caliber pistol bullet into the bore of a .50-caliber rifle. Early sabots were often made of wood (circa 1800s) and the earliest known form of a sabot was the cloth patch used on a patched round ball.

Set trigger - Set triggers have been offered in two forms, double-set and single-set. A double-set trigger features a two-trigger arrangement. By first pulling the "set" (normally the rear trigger), the front trigger requires extremely light pressure to drop the hammer. Most single-set triggers require that the trigger first be pushed forward into the "set" position, which in turn lightens the amount of trigger pull needed to drop the hammer tremendously. Most are adjustable and can be set less than a pound.

Short starter - A loading accessory which consists of a short five- or six-inch rod fitted to a round or flat palm-fitting handle and used for starting a muzzleloading projectile into the bore.

Slow-twist rifling - This term is used to distinguish those rifles which have been rifled for shooting the patched round ball. Slow twist barrels are those with rifling which spin with a one-turn-in-60 to -72 inches rate of twist. These slower twists offer less resistance to the patched ball and generally provide the best accuracy.

Swaged bullet/ball - A muzzleloading projectile which has been formed by a swaging process instead of being cast. A swaged ball or bullet is formed by forcing pure lead into a precision die under great hydraulic pressure. Swaged projectiles are free of any sprue marks.

Tenon - A small metal loop or piece of flat metal attached to the bottom of a muzzleloader's barrel through which a flat key or pin is used to attach the barrel to the forestock.

Thimble - The metal ferrules located along the bottom of the barrel and often on the stock which hold the ramrod in place.

• *What does he know that you don't know, and vice versa? That is the core of the challenge. Photo by Gary Clancy.*

Chapter 2

Hunting The Third Season

The overgrown hay field stretching out in front of Brent Hunt's tree stand was covered with a heavy frost that, in the early morning light, looked almost like a new layer of snow. It was a sight that this South Carolina native normally didn't see during the whitetail season in his home state. Brent had made the long drive to sample northern Missouri's fabled big whitetail hunting.

Somewhere along the hardwood covered ridge running behind him, a flock of turkeys raised a ruckus as they flew down from their roosts just as the first light of a warming sun filtered through the bare oaks. Several minutes later, a doe and two fawns appeared at the far end of the opening, right where an old field road connected this particular field with another, then another and another.

It had been several years since hay had been cut and baled here. Still, deer from the surrounding hardwoods relied heavily on volunteer clover which still sprouted beneath the canopy of overgrown, taller weeds. The clover was a supplement to their steady diet of acorns and timber browse.

The previous day, Brent had located a well-used scrape within yards of where the old doe and her fawns were standing. Another, even larger scrape was located less than 10 yards from the tree where he had located his portable stand. To make the area even more appealing, there were dozens of sizeable rubs and smaller scrapes nearly ringing the field.

While the old whitetail doe probably had entered this field on hundreds of occasions, she still eased into the open expanse with that nervousness only a whitetail can exhibit. She took a few steps forward, stomped her front feet several times, then took a few more steps forward. She repeated the antic several times, until she was 40 yards from the edge of the hardwoods. Finally, she relaxed and began feeding on the clover undergrowth.

Brent was busy watching the three deer slowly browse across the opening when the sound of crunching leaves somewhere behind him caught his ear. Careful not to move so fast as to draw attention from the doe and fawns, he eased around in his stand to try to locate the source of the crunching.

A big doe materialized from the shadows of a small pond dam 75 yards away. The deer stood looking back for several minutes before moving on but stopped several more times in less than 30 yards to look back

• Brent Hunt with his Missouri eight-pointer, dropped cleanly with a single shot from his in-line percussion muzzleloader.

in the direction from which she had just come. There had to be a buck following.

The doe and fawns were now less than 40 yards directly in front of Brent's stand, so he had to use extreme caution in bringing up his .50-caliber rifle. Just as he rested the forearm of the in-line percussion muzzleloader on a small branch which offered a convenient rest, a good eight-point buck stepped from out of the pond dam's shadow. Instead of following the doe, the buck made his way directly to one of the scrapes Brent had located the previous day.

As the deer nosed the bare spot on the ground just 60 yards away, Brent contemplated taking the shot, but the buck still was facing him more than it should be for the best possible bullet placement. However, Brent already had slipped off the sliding side safety and visually made sure the secondary safety at the rear of the plunger style hammer was threaded all the way back into the "fire" position.

The big bodied buck spotted the deer in the field and for a second acted as if he were going to join them. Instead, the buck turned to rejoin the single doe now standing in the open timber 40 yards from Brent. When the buck eased through an opening in the trees, Brent settled the crosshairs of his scope just to the rear of the whitetail's front shoulder and gently applied pressure to the trigger. The rifle belched fire and smoke. At the shot, the buck lunged forward, ran a few yards and went down.

Like millions of whitetail deer hunters today, Brent Hunt, the owner of Trophy Whitetail Products, has turned to muzzleloading to cash in on bonus whitetail deer hunting opportunities. There is good reason why!

Hunting with a muzzleloader is just now going through the same stages of development archery experienced with the introduction of the compound bow during the early 1970s. Back then, many traditional longbow and recurve bow shooters didn't like the new mechanical contraptions. They felt they weren't bows, and that they threatened to change the sport of bowhunting. Change bowhunting the compound did!

I've always been one of those hunters who likes to go afield with the most efficient arm available, whether it is a muzzleloader or a bow. I jumped on the compound bow bandwagon the first time I saw one of the original Allen compounds and went home from that show with one tucked under my arm. Many of the shops I went into back in 1972 to pick up accessories for my new-fangled "banjo" bow literally threw me out, saying they wanted nothing to do with such equipment. Less than four years later these same shops were selling more compounds than long or recurve bows. Today, the number of archers who head for the deer woods with a compound bow account for more than 90 percent of all bowhunters.

Just as the traditional bowhunter of more than two decades ago, the traditional muzzleloading shooter also has felt somewhat threatened by the introduction of today's ultra-modern-looking percussion in-line rifles. The feeling is that they are just too efficient and too accurate. So much so, the traditionalists feel, the average shooter just coming into the sport will be tempted to push the effective range of muzzleloading beyond where black powder ballistics will insure good clean kills on big game.

Truth is, as modern as many of the in-line hunting rigs may appear, they are still

• *Muzzleloading has drawn hunters from the ranks of archery and modern firearms hunters. Bonus or additional hunting opportunities are the lure, making them three-season hunters.*

• Game managers today are faced with underharvest in many areas. Whitetail herds are at an all-time high. Special seasons and larger bag limits help control the herd. Tom Fegely photo.

bound by the limited ballistics of black powder or Pyrodex powders. The powder and ball (bullet) do not know what type ignition sent it down the barrel; black powder ballistics are black powder ballistics. When taking a shot, it's the hunter's ethics which guide whether or not the animal is in range. That applies to hunting with a bow, a centerfire rifle or shotgun, or a muzzleloader.

Back 20 to 25 years ago when the first of today's muzzleloading deer and other big game seasons first began to be established, these seasons were established to provide hunters with an opportunity to experience what it was like to hunt with a firearm design dating from the days of our forefathers. However, just 20 years ago game managers in most states were still concerned about an overharvest of game, even the whitetail deer. Close tabs had to be kept on hunter numbers in the different seasons to insure that the resource was not taxed.

Today, game managers are faced with a totally different problem, and that's the underharvest of many big game species. In most regions of the country, whitetail herds are at an all-time high. In fact, in many suburban areas the whitetail population is so great the animals are reaching the point of being classified as pests. Today, game departments are relying on special muzzleloading deer and other big game seasons as a bonafide management tool to keep a burgeoning game population in check with available habitat.

As this was written, only a few states did not have a separate muzzleloading season. In most states, seasons which were established during the 1970s or early 1980s have been greatly expanded due to fast growing popularity and the need for additional deer harvest.

Opportunities for the muzzleloading hunter look extremely bright. In a number of states the army of orange coated hunters who take to the deer woods for the general firearm season already number from 500,000 to as many as 1,000,000. With so many hunters afield for a 10 day to two week season, it's unlikely that game departments will look at extending those seasons in order to increase the harvest. They're already controlling as many people as they can

• *The promise of uncrowded hunting is one of the biggest draws of special muzzleloading seasons.*

handle for as long a period as feasible. Then, on the other hand, the archery seasons are already about as liberal as most states can make them, allowing the hunter to tag several deer in some states and giving him upward of three months to do so.

As deer herds continue to grow, I'm sure we'll see more and more game departments turn to muzzleloader seasons and hunts as a serious game management tool. Michigan is currently recognized as the number one muzzleloading state. During this state's December muzzleloader whitetail season as many as 150,000 to 160,000 dedicated deer hunters pick up a muzzleloader for one more shot at putting venison in the freezer. In Pennsylvania, more than 100,000 black powder burners annually have taken part in that state's muzzleloader whitetail season for more than a decade. In a number of other states, as many as 60,000 to 80,000 deer hunters have turned to a muzzleloader to extend their hunting season.

While this may seem like a lot of hunters, in each case the number of muzzleloading hunters afield in a given state still normally represents far less than 10 percent of the deer hunters who participate in the general firearm season. The promise of uncrowded hunting is one of the biggest draws of special muzzleloading seasons.

Today's black powder shooter is a hunter. He's turned to packing a muzzleloader for an entirely different reason than the shooter who got into muzzleloading during the late 1960s or early 1970s. Today's black powder shooter hasn't turned to muzzleloading just to relive the past or to try hunting with an old-fashioned frontloading rifle such as that carried by our forefathers. The modern day Daniel Boone is out there to hunt deer, and he's turned to muzzleloading in order to cash in on the growing opportunities of the muzzleloader "third season" hunts.

Brent Hunt has discovered the enjoyment of hunting with a muzzleloader and he ... like many people ... has come to realize that in some regions the special muzzleloading hunts offer the trophy buck hunter his best chance to tag a bragging-size whitetail. Like more and more of today's big buck hunters, Brent is finding he's doing more travelling to other states to take part in muzzleloader whitetail hunts.

While Brent enjoys the challenge of hunting with a muzzleloader, he nevertheless relies on a percussion, in-line model, the most efficient muzzleloading rifle design available today. This style of frontloader is a far cry from the traditionally-styled reproduction muzzleloading rifles which flooded the market through the 1970s. In fact, his rifle, built by Modern Muzzleloading, has a high-tech composite thumbhole stock which makes it even more modern looking. Where legal, Brent also relies on a good variable-power scope to make this rifle even better suited for taking shots out to and slightly past 150 yards.

The effectiveness, reliability, accuracy and familiar feel of the modern in-line rifles have done as much to bring new shooters into muzzleloading as has the lure of the bonus hunting seasons. These rifles have the feel and balance of the modern centerfire rifles most new black powder hunters grew up with. For many of those new to the sport, traditionally-styled black powder rifles offered poor balance, heavy weight, an awkward feel and unfamiliar features....most or all of which left them cold.

Not everyone goes this far in modernizing the muzzleloading hunting rifle. However, few hunters today head out with an exact copy of a Pennsylvania long rifle, especially if it's a flintlock. While all of us who hunt with the more modern muzzleloading hunting rigs can admire and appreciate the hunter who accepts such a challenge, we're all happy that muzzleloading regulations are becoming more and more relaxed, giving us the free-

• *The effectiveness, reliability, accuracy and familiar feel of the modern in-line rifles have done as much to bring new shooters into muzzleloading as has the lure of the bonus seasons.*

• *This black powder burner used a Thompson/Center Hawken to tag his buck.*

dom of choice of just how modern a frontloader we can hunt with.

I first noticed the trend to shorter, more practical hunting designs during the mid 1970s. Fewer and fewer of the muzzleloading hunters I ran into on special hunts during the late 1970s relied on models with barrels exceeding 30 inches. A hunt on the Wattensaw Wildlife Management Area east of Little Rock, Arkansas, in 1978 pretty well exemplified the changing trend to shorter barrels.

Early the first morning of the hunt, I had been lucky enough to score on a nice eight-pointer. I was the guest of the management area manager, and he wanted me to spend some time with him visiting the other camps and polling some of the hunters to learn just what everyone was hunting with and the loads they were using. In all, we talked with an even 100 hunters over three days.

We were amazed to find that more than 80 percent of the hunters we spoke with were hunting with the Thompson/Center Hawken rifle. Of these, 80 percent were of percussion persuasion and the preferred caliber ran about 50/50 for the .45 and .50 caliber bores. When this survey was taken, Thompson/Center had introduced the rifle in .54 caliber just a couple of months earlier. We weren't too surprised to run into only one hunter using the rifle in that caliber. Not too surprisingly, the second most popular model we encountered was the Thompson/Center Renegade in .54 caliber. The Hawken features a 28-inch barrel, while the Renegade sports an even shorter 26-inch barrel.

We actually ran into only six hunters who were packing something other than a Thompson/Center-built muzzleloader. A couple of hunters who had travelled to central Arkansas from western Tennessee for this hunt were carrying custom built flintlock long rifles, three were packing rifles imported by Connecticut Valley Arms, and one a Dixie Gun Works long rifle.

The year I conducted this survey the Arkansas Game & Fish Commission sold in the neighborhood of 24,000 muzzleloading permits. If hunters statewide were carrying Thompson/Center rifles in the same ratio, it would mean that more than 19,000 Thompson/Center Hawkens were being used, showing a real preference for a shorter barrel length and faster handling muzzleloader design. (Today, the Arkansas Game & Fish Commission estimates as many as 65,000 hunters go afield with a muzzleloading rifle.)

THE CHANGE-OVER BEGAN

On another hunt nearly 15 years later, I was able to see an even more amazing change in the type of muzzleloader preferred. That hunt took place on a corporate-owned farm in western Kentucky along the Ohio River. The 13,000 acre piece of property boasted a whitetail population of more than 3,000. To keep the deer herd in check, the company conducts four hunts a year, allowing 100 hunters on each. Each hunter is allowed to harvest a buck and a doe. The success rate runs upward of 90 percent and there is considerable competi-

• *Black powder as you want it — traditional gear or more-modern, any style of hunting, all types of seasons and hunting conditions, alone or in a group. It's a wide-open field today, with few exceptions. Right, hunting with a flintlock rifle may conjur visions of Daniel Boone or Davy Crockett, but a flintlock is extremely difficult to master. Be practical with your decision on which style to purchase. Photo at right by Tom Fegely. Photo below by Gary Clancy.*

• *Muzzleloader hunter, high in a ladder stand, covers a Georgia buck he took. Photo by Richard P. Smith.*

tion for permits, even though two hunts are muzzleloader only.

I had no problem filling my two tags on the first day of the hunt. In fact, by noon I had seen more than 100 deer and had taken my doe early in the morning and my buck just before noon.

I spent the rest of the time hanging around the check station or talking with hunters I ran into along the gravel roads that laced the property. I must have chatted with around 50 of the 100 hunters on the farm for the weekend hunt. All but three were using percussion in-line Knight rifles. One of the three who weren't was using a Connecticut Valley Arms "Apollo" percussion in-line rifle. The other two were relying on Thompson/Center Hawken rifles.

Muzzleloading, and more specifically hunting with a muzzleloader, has come a long way since the rebirth of black powder shooting sports in the late 1950s. With whitetail herds continuing to grow in most regions of the country, we're bound to see game departments rely more heavily on muzzleloading seasons to manage deer population levels. This simply means bonus hunting for the deer hunter who has already added muzzleloading to his schedule of archery and modern firearms whitetail hunts. With the added hunting opportunities, we'll more than likely continue to see new hunters make the move to muzzleloading.

Whether you decide to hunt with a rifle of traditional design or with one of today's modern in-line ignition muzzleloaders, taking a whitetail buck with a slow-to-load frontloading rifle is a good feeling. It takes a great deal of devotion to spend days in a treestand knowing you have just one good shot, but that's the satisfaction of hunting with a muzzleloader — having the confidence in yourself and your rifle to make that shot count when the time comes.

Chapter 3

Muzzleloading Enters A New Era

In the mid 1950s, a small clan of muzzleloading shooters began to rekindle interest in shooting frontloading guns. Their efforts were hampered by the fact that the only muzzleloaders available were either shootable originals dating from centuries past or costly custom built copies of those guns.

That was until an enterprising young Tennessean named Turner Kirkland introduced what was the first of what has come to be known as "reproduction" muzzleloaders. A gun collector who had an eye for originals of the "Kentucky rifle" design, Kirkland studied the more than 100 originals in his collection. He noted the features which were most evident on the guns, then set out to design his modern copy.

The rifle which eventually was built in Belgium was a .40-caliber full stock Kentucky rifle with a 40-inch barrel. At best, the new longrifle was a facsimile of the originals it was supposed to have copied. However, it served its purpose, for it offered a safe, serviceable and accurate modern-made muzzleloader for about $100.

Dixie Gun Works first offered their .40 caliber "Squirrel Rifle" in the mail order firm's 1956 catalog. The rifle was a success in terms of setting the stage for a whole new shooting industry to develop in this country. However, in terms of rifles actually sold, the Dixie Kentucky Rifle, as it later became known, saw a total production of less than 25,000. The rifle was discontinued in 1978.

When you look back at the guns which followed the Dixie Gun Works longrifle, you have to remember that the primary reason for the shooter of that time to take up muzzleloading was purely a historic or nostalgic one. For a fast-growing number of Americans, muzzleloading guns served as a hands-on link to the taming of our eastern mountains, the westward expansion, the carefree days of the fur trade era, our early conflicts with the British, or even our very own Civil War.

Civil War buff Val Forgett capitalized on the centennial of the war by introducing several near exact copies of the percussion revolvers carried during the conflict. The most successful of the Italian made reproductions was a copy of the Colt Model 1851 Navy revolver. The .36-caliber percussion handgun was so successful that Forgett named his newly founded company Navy Arms. Another of the Italian-manufactured black powder guns which was immediately

• Dixie Gun Works founder Turner Kirkland with some of the originals in his collection which were used to help design the very first "reproduction" muzzleloader.

successful for him was a copy of the .58 caliber Remington Zouave rifled musket. With all of the big gun's brass barrel bands, nose cap and butt plate, historians often refer to the musket as the most colorful of all Civil War long guns.

During the early 1960s, shooters began to make new demands on muzzleloading gun suppliers. Around the country, a few states had established seasons which allowed muzzleloaders only, or seasons which were termed "primitive weapons" hunts which allowed bow, crossbow, or muzzleloaders only. It should be noted that many states then also allowed a muzzleloader to be carried during the general firearm deer and other big game seasons, as long as a frontloader met specified minimum requirements, especially minimum bore sizes.

In 1963, Dixie Gun Works upped the bore size of their "Squirrel Rifle" to .45 caliber and redubbed the long gun the Dixie Kentucky Rifle. The larger bore size better met the needs of the hunter who wanted to use the rifle on deer, while still providing the budget minded shooter a reasonably economical bore size to shoot. (Note: The author purchased his first muzzleloading rifle in 1964, a .45 caliber Dixie Kentucky Rifle, for $125.)

Two other entries to the muzzleloading marketplace in 1963 targeted the black powder deer hunter. One was a sporterized version of the Navy Arms .58 caliber Zouave rifled musket, known as the "Buffalo Hunter". The gun was reminiscent of the chopped and sporterized originals which followed the Civil War, as soldiers returned home and found they had to feed their families from what they could harvest from the woods and fields.

The other gun was the Hopkins & Allen underhammer rifle from Numrich Arms. While the .45 caliber frontloader would hardly ever win a beauty contest, the rifle did one thing better than any other muzzleloader on the market. It allowed a shooter to get into muzzleloading for about what it cost to purchase a .22 semi-auto rifle.

At that time, Dixie and Navy Arms were both selling their muzzleloading deer rifles for just over $100. Numrich Arms sold their .45 caliber Hopkins & Allen underhammer for $49.95, and it came with a powder flask, powder, balls, patches and percussion caps. This was everything a shooter needed to get started, for half of what the others were charging.

The growing demand for a handy and effective muzzleloading big game rifle led to the introduction in 1971 of the most successful of today's reproduction guns. In every business, they say timing is everything, and the timing of Thompson/Center Arms' introduction of their half-stocked Hawken rifle couldn't have been better.

Originally offered in a choice of .45 or .50 caliber (the .54-caliber version came later), the Thompson/Center Hawken represented the first modern-built muzzleloading rifle that had been designed totally around the big game hunter's needs.

The 28-inch barrel immediately appealed to the hunter who often found himself shooting from a cramped treestand or easing through heavy cover. The rifle also came with a good quality set of sights, with a rear sight that easily adjusted for both windage and elevation. Thompson/Center was also the first reproduction manufacturer to utilize reliable coil springs inside the lock instead of traditional flat or V-springs. The mechanisms were so trouble free that the manufacturer backed the Hawken rifle with a "lifetime warranty", the first for the muzzleloading industry.

When Warren Center sat down to design and develop the Thompson/Center Hawken rifle, along with it he also designed a hard-hitting big game bullet for the muzzle loader. That bullet was the Thompson/Center "Maxi-Ball".

This great hunk of lead weighs nearly twice that of a round ball for the same caliber rifle. A .45 caliber Maxi-Ball tips the

• *Val Forgett of Navy Arms played an instrumental role in bringing high quality modern-made muzzleloaders to a growing number of black powder shooters and hunters.*

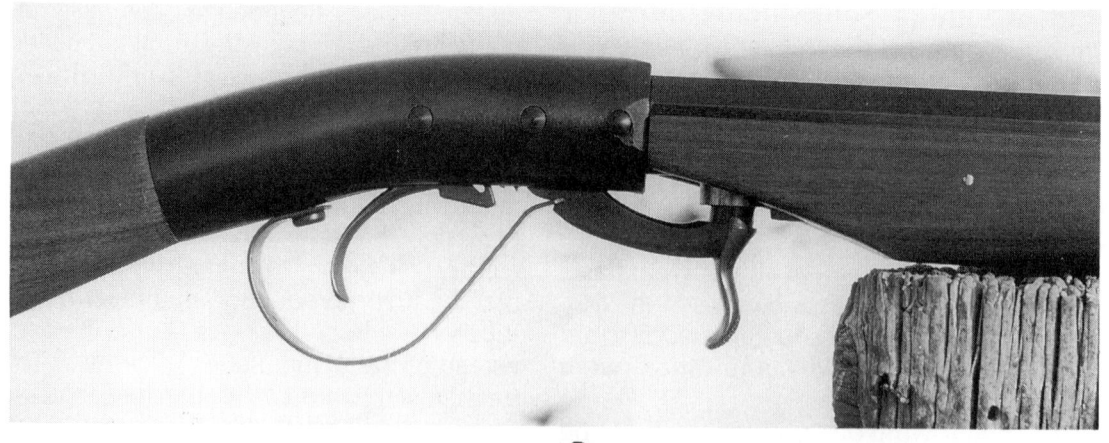

• The inexpensive Hopkins & Allen underhammer rifles of the 1960s brought a large number of shooters into the sport by making black powder shooting affordable.

• The Navy Arms "Buffalo Hunter" was one of the first serious muzzleloading hunting rifles.

scales at 240 grains, compared to 128 grains for a .440-inch diameter round ball fired in most .45 caliber rifles. A .50 caliber Maxi weighs a whopping 370 grains, more than twice the weight of a 178 grain .490-inch round ball for the same caliber rifle.

With a length nearly twice its diameter, the Maxi-Ball required a considerable amount of spin on the bullet to stabilize it in flight. Since the conical slug is loaded without patching, relying on light engravement by the rifling when loaded, the rifling cannot be very deep. The Hawken was designed with shallow groove rifling which spun with a fast (for the time) one turn in 48 inches. This was a radical change from a round ball rifle's bore.

The flashy brass mounted stock of the Thompson/Center rifle was a far cry from duplicating the original Hawken rifles that were built in St. Louis during the heyday of the western fur trade, throughout the 1830s and 1840s. Many traditional muzzleloading shooters who demanded authenticity in the rifles they hunted with took exception to Thompson/Center calling their very modern side-hammer muzzleloader a Hawken.

Still, the Thompson/Center Hawken quickly became the best selling reproduction on the market. At about the same time, a motion picture titled "Jeremiah Johnson", starring Robert Redford, depicted the Hawken rifle as the rifle of choice by the mountain man of the 1840s. The timing was

• *The Thompson/Center Hawken rifle, left, has been the number one selling muzzleloader for more than two decades.*

• *The popularity of the Thompson/Center Hawken spurred the introduction of other half-stock hunting rifles. Shown here is another Thompson/Center model, the Renegade.*

perfect, and Thompson/Center's Hawken became a common household name among black powder shooters. To date, right at 1,000,000 of the rifles have been sold in factory finished and kit form.

The popularity of the half-stock Hawken rifle spurred the introduction of other similarly designed rifles. Even Thompson/Center took advantage of the short half-stock's wide acceptance and introduced several other similarly designed models. The firm's Renegade model, introduced in 1974, and New Englander, which hit the market in 1985, have both been great sellers. Both of these rifles have been designed even more for the serious big game hunter, eliminating flashy brass ornamentation and featuring a comfortable flat shotgun style buttplate instead of the traditional crescent buttplate found on the Hawken model.

Dixie Gun Works, Navy Arms, Lyman, Connecticut Valley Arms and a number of other United States companies have all imported from Italy and Spain a wide range of half-stock rifles of the so-called "Hawken" styling. Some of these guns are of more authentic design than others. Even so, they all share one trait, and that is the shorter length and fast handling characteristics.

> *The 1970s established the half-stock preference and that bore sizes of .45 or smaller were ineffective on deer and other big game*

The middle to late '70s not only established the half-stock as the choice of black powder hunters, the period also established that bore sizes of .45 and smaller were ineffective on deer and other big game. Out of this period grew a lopsided love affair with rifles of .50 caliber. A relatively large number of shooters and hunters west of the Mississippi tended to stick with the slightly bigger .54-caliber rifles, contending that they delivered more knockdown power for game as big as elk. Still, for every .54 and larger big bore, or .45 and smaller caliber rifle sold during the late 1970's, four or five times as many half-inch bored frontloaders left dealer shelves.

While the early muzzleloading seasons had been designed as "opportunity" seasons to give modern day hunters a taste of what it was like to hunt in the past, the longer and more liberal muzzleloading deer seasons which became more common by the mid 1980s were definitely intended as "harvest" seasons. Muzzleloading had begun its transition from a nostalgic or historic study to a true hunting sport. In all but a few whitetail states, the muzzleloader deer seasons became honest "third season" hunting opportunities.

The lure of these seasons caused many modern firearm hunters to take a serious look at hunting with a muzzleloading rifle. In many states, muzzleloader seasons not only offered the dedicated deer hunter an opportunity to double or even triple his hunting time, in many they also allowed him to harvest additional game.

In many parts of the country, muzzleloader hunts are held prior to the general firearm deer hunts, or can take place at the peak of the breeding period. A rut-crazed big buck that hasn't been pressured can be a much easier quarry than the same deer once hundreds of thousands of centerfire rifle-toting deer hunters take to the woods. Even where these seasons take place following the firearm seasons, the less crowded hunting conditions make for a more enjoyable hunt.

To take full advantage of these opportunities, today's black powder hunter is turning to a new breed of muzzleloading hunting rifle, with designs which stray farther and farther from traditional muzzleloading designs. **Today's muzzleloading hunter relies on as modern a muzzleloader as the law will allow. A number of these guns are capable of accuracy which will rival many centerfire rifles at 100 or even 150 yards.**

The rifle which quickly established new standards for a serious muzzleloading hunting rifle was the Knight MK-85. The introduction of this rifle in 1985 proved that a frontloading rifle didn't have to look, handle or perform like the old-fashioned muzzleloading rifles hunters had become accustomed to shooting.

The heart of this modernistic muzzleloader is the rifle's efficient, in-line ignition system. Even from only a short distance away, this "action" looks much like the bolt of the action of a modern centerfire semi-auto. Actually, what looks like the bolt of the action is the rifle's plunger style hammer riding inside the MK-85's receiver.

This system places the nipple squarely in the rear center of the breechplug, which in turn threads directly into the rear of the barrel. A hollowed recess in the face of the breechplug allows the powder charge to come tight to the bottom of the nipple. Fire from an exploding No. 11 percussion cap

• *This is the rifle which brought muzzleloading into the 21st Century....the Knight MK-85. Rifle shown is an early version.*

reaches the powder charge in a direct path for exceptionally fast and positive ignition.

A unique feature of the MK-85 is the rifle's dual safety system. The primary safety is a standard thumb-operated side safety which locks the rifle's adjustable trigger when in the rear "on" position. The secondary safety is in the form of a knurled nut at the rear of the plunger hammer. When the hammer is cocked back, this nut can be threaded forward to form an effective hammer block. Even if the trigger is pulled and the hammer falls, the forward face of this safety will bottom out against the rear of the receiver, keeping the hammer face nearly a half-inch away from the capped nipple.

Modern Muzzleloading, the manufacturer of the Knight MK-85, builds this rifle with a long list of other features which appeal to today's hunter. The stock lines of this rifle are similar to those of a bolt-action centerfire Ruger Model 77 or Remington Model 700. The maker now offers the rifle with a choice of walnut, laminated or composite stock. The most avant-garde of the versions available is the "Knight Hawk" model, which comes with an ultra-modern, thumbhole, composite stock. Even the most open minded traditional muzzleloader shooter will have a difficult time accepting this rifle as a muzzleloader, especially the stainless steel variation!

Even so, the hunter looking for the highest level of efficiency and accuracy from a hunting muzzleloader is finding the MK-85 rifle very much to his liking. Here is a rifle that can print 1-1/2-inch groups at a hundred yards, right out of the box.

Modern Muzzleloading also has been largely responsible for destroying the myth that it took at least a 28- or 30-inch barrel to get a muzzleloading rifle to shoot accurately. The longest barrel length they offer is 24 inches, while barrels of 22 and 20 inches are also available. Each comes precision cut rifled with eight lands and grooves which spiral with an extremely fast one-turn-in-28 inches rate of twist. This definitely is a rifle designed for shooting conical bullets and not the patched round ball.

However, when shooting a rifle of such modern technology, it's something of a step

• *Plastic sabots have done as much to revolutionize the sport of muzzleloading as has any rifle introduced in the past 30 years.*

backward to shoot anything but a projectile, or rather a projectile system, that's equally modern. While the Knight rifle shoots well with a variety of soft pure lead conical bullets, this rifle really performs when stuffed with plastic sabot and any of a wide range of modern .44- and .45-caliber jacketed pistol bullets in the .50- and .54-caliber rifles.

Muzzleload Magnum Products has done its share of changing how today's shooter looks at muzzleloading, and all this company makes is a small plastic sabot. **As simple as these tiny plastic cups may seem, they have done as much to revolutionize the sport of muzzleloading as has any rifle introduced in the past 30 years.**

The sabots allow today's black powder hunter to load and shoot several hundred smaller diameter pistol bullets in their larger bored hunting rifles. The sabot serves much the same purpose of the patch used to fire a round ball. The sabot takes up the difference between the larger bore and smaller bullet, while at the same time transferring the spin of the rifling to the bullet. The sabot drops away from the bullet only a few yards from the muzzle, while the bullet travels on to the target...very accurately.

This system gives you a much wider range of bullet weights, from light weights of about 180 grains to heavy weights of more than 400 grains, and lets you better tailor a load to the game being hunted. Modern Muzzleloading, Hornady Manufacturing and Thompson/Center now market sabots of their own, as well.

It's impossible for a rifle to be successful and remain the only rifle of its type or style on the market. Thompson/Center's Hawken proved that in the early 1970s, and the Knight percussion in-line rifle proved it again in the mid-1980s. There presently are a number of similarly designed rifles available. One of the first to follow the Knight MK-85 was the Apollo from Connecticut Valley Arms. A more recent introduction has been the Thompson/Center Thunder

Hawk. While neither is built with all the features of the Knight rifle, both feature modern looks and feel, fast twist rifling for superior accuracy with conical and saboted bullets, and efficient in-line ignition systems.

So where does muzzleloading go from here? Modern Muzzleloading already has begun to offer frontloaders for the 21st Century with the introduction of their "Magnum Elite". This rifle eliminates the nipple and percussion cap. Instead, the rifle utilizes a chambered plastic capsule and large rifle primer for ignition, which is spontaneous. Not only does the much hotter flame from a large rifle or magnum large rifle primer give more sure-fire ignition, it also gives ignition of the powder charge at the same millisecond from shot to shot, which in turn gives tighter groups downrange. Like archery, muzzleloading will continue to see more and more modern technology employed and today's frontloading hunting guns will become more efficient.

For some, the modern looks of the in-line rifles destroy the feel of hunting with a muzzleloader. Yet, they like the idea of shooting and hunting with saboted bullets, and the exceptionally short, handy barrel lengths. For these shooters, there are several "hybrids" which combine traditional side-hammer styling with one of the high-tech fast twist barrels. Easily the most popular of these has been the short 21-inch barreled White Mountain Carbine from Thompson/Center. Just slightly more modern in appearance is the same company's Scout carbine, an in-line which features an external, traditionally-styled hammer. Both of these rifles feature fast one-turn-in-20 inches rifling twists.

It doesn't seem to matter if the rifle is traditionally styled, modern, or somewhere in between, the sight of a scope aboard a muzzleloading hunting rifle is becoming more commonplace. In recent years, the number of states which allow the use of telescopic sights aboard a frontloading rifle has nearly doubled.

As you can see, nostalgia plays a diminishing role in the reasons shooters pick up a muzzleloader for the first time. Muzzleloading is just now entering the same stage of interest and development which archery experienced during the 1970s. In a sense, today's modern in-line rifles are the "compound bows" of the muzzleloading sport. Many traditionalists are sure to resist them, while the black powder shooter who

● *The Connecticut Valley Arms "Apollo" was one of the first in-line percussion rifles to cash in on the popularity of the "modern" muzzleloading concept established by the Knight rifles.*

has turned to muzzleloading solely to cash in on bonus hunting provided by special muzzleloading seasons will welcome the guns with open arms. Whether you agree with in-line ignition systems, modern looks, fast twist rifling and saboted bullets, or whether you don't, they're here to stay.

Muzzleloading is a sport which can be as primitive and challenging as you want it to be, or as modern and efficient as technology will allow. Fortunately, as the sport moves into a new era, today's shooter enjoys the freedom to choose the direction he or she will take.

Chapter 4

Selecting A Muzzleloading Deer Rifle

Never before has the selection of well built muzzleloading hunting rifles been better. With such a variety of frontloading guns to choose from, the beginning black powder hunter has to be just a little bewildered when trying to decide which model or models best fit/ his or her needs. Before jumping right in and buying the first rifle looked at, the smart shooter should first ask a few questions.

What price range can I afford?

While price is definitely a factor, never settle for lesser quality just to save a few bucks. There are some great frontloading hunting rifles available in just about all price ranges.

Thompson/Center's Hawken rifle has been a standard setter for rifles of that design ever since the gun was first introduced in the early 1970s. Backed with a lifetime warranty, this is one well-built, traditionally-styled black powder rifle for the hunter who wants to muzzleload for whitetails and have a bit of history carried on his shoulder. For some, however, this rifle will be outside the budget.

Still, there are other well-built models of Hawken styling with price tags roughly half that of the Thompson/Center rifle. They may not come with a lifetime warranty, and they may not display the fit and finish of the Thompson/Center Hawken, but some of these rifles will perform right along with the higher priced rifle.

Major outdoor products catalog companies like Bass Pro Shops, Cabela's and Gander Mountain offer private label "Hawken" rifles which for the most part are great buys. These guns are built for these catalogers by known names in the muzzleloading industry, such as Connecticut Valley Arms and Traditions, Inc.

Percussion in-line rifles have won an undeserving reputation for being high priced. Sure, top of the line models like the stainless steel White Super Model 91 and the Knight MK-85 "Knight Hawk" have premium price tags. They should, since they are well built, precision muzzleloaders incorporating the best components available today. However, there are efficient in-line ignition rifles which retail for about a third of what these top-of-the-line models sell for.

Modern Muzzleloading's Wolverine is one of these rifles. Here is a no-nonsense .50 caliber in-line hunting rifle built without all the expensive frills. Still, this rifle is built with a top quality Green Mountain cut-

• Buy the best quality muzzleloading rifle you can afford. The cost is an investment, not an expense. The author took this Illinois buck with a .50 caliber Dixie Hawken.

• The rifle you're hoping to buy must meet regulations in the state(s) you plan to hunt. That may be bore size, barrel length, legal projectiles or ignition system. Photo by Betty Lou Fegely.

rifled barrel, fully adjustable trigger, removable stainless steel breech plug for easy cleaning from the breech end of the barrel, and the Knight patented double safety system. All of this is mounted on a tough, plastic, injection molded stock.

Does the rifle I'm thinking about buying meet muzzleloading regulations of the state I plan to hunt?

Some states impose certain requirements on a muzzleloading big game rifle. Before shucking out dollars for a rifle which may or may not meet these regulations, take time to check. Be sure of regulations which may define a minimum bore size, barrel length required, legal projectiles and even the type of ignition system. Most states require a minimum bore size of around .38 to .40 caliber, although today's serious whitetail hunter would be much better off selecting a rifle of at least .50 caliber. Check the chapters of this book dealing with ballistics for a better idea of what to expect from a frontloading deer rifle.

One of the more popular muzzleloading deer seasons in the country takes place in Pennsylvania, where more

• Percussion is more moisture-forgiving than flint ignition, but for added percussion protection, CVA's cap protector keeps water from seeping into the cap-ignition area. Photo by Betty Lou Fegely.

• Another simple solution to keeping a percussion cap dry during a rainy hunt is to coat the outside edges with bowstring wax.

than 100,000 black powder burners take to the deer woods each winter. As this was written, hunters in this state are required to use a flintlock rifle and patched round ball only. However, as with many other states where the sport of hunting with a muzzleloader has matured in recent years, there is a major push to legalize percussion rifles for the Pennsylvania muzzleloading season. If enough hunters want the change, it will happen.

Unless certain state regulations specify flint ignition, the beginning muzzleloading deer hunter is better off starting with a percussion rifle. Many muzzleloaders who purchased a flint rifle at the outset of their new hunting challenge became frustrated trying to master the rifle and simply give up. Worse yet, some carry the rifles into the field anyway, even though they realize they don't know how to shoot the rifle confidently enough to insure a clean kill, if and when the time comes.

The percussion ignition system is a lot more forgiving than flint ignition, especially in damp weather. Once a beginning muzzleloading shooter has mastered the loading and shooting of a percussion ignition system, he can always make the slow but confident transition to flint if he wants. Some of today's reproduction rifles can be switched easily from percussion ignition to flint ignition in minutes -- and at a fraction of the cost of buying a new rifle.

What caliber is best for hunting whitetails and other big game?

If the round ball is the chosen projectile, then you need to concentrate on those rifles with deeply cut rifling grooves which spin with a slow one-turn-in-60 to 66 inches. Due to the inefficiency of a patched round ball on deer-sized game beyond 50 yards, the serious muzzleloading whitetail hunter shouldn't consider anything smaller than a .50 caliber rifle, if that's the projectile you want to shoot.

On the other hand, if a conical bullet or saboted handgun bullet is to be loaded and shot, rifles of .45 caliber will still do the job on deer and similarly-sized game when loaded with a hefty powder charge behind a bullet of 200 to 300 grains. However, you will have to concentrate on those models which are rifled with faster one-turn-in-20

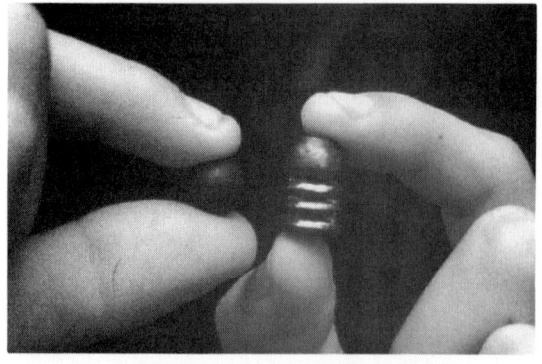

• Both of these projectiles are for shooting from a .50 caliber muzzleloader. The 350-grain Thompson/Center Maxi-Hunter, at right, weighs nearly twice as much as the .490" round ball.

• Keep in mind the type of projectile you intend to shoot and hunt with. Conicals like the big Thompson/Center Maxi-Ball deliver much more punch than a patched round ball.

to 32 inches rate of twist.

Today, after having taken more than 130 big game animals with muzzleloading guns, I've come to regard the .50 caliber frontloaders as the optimum bore size for hunting big game, especially when loaded with any of the heavier conical bullets and saboted handgun bullets. In fact, the .50 caliber is ballistically superior to the slightly larger .54 caliber rifles in every instance except one...when the rifles are loaded with a patched round ball.

The .50 caliber will do anything the .54 caliber can do. Now, I know this statement has probably already stirred up the dandruff on a few of you big bore fans. If so, this next statement may have you seeing double. That is, that **the .50 caliber is actually ballistically superior to the .54 caliber.**

Surely, some of you are now wondering just how much I know about shooting muzzleloaders after that claim. Everyone knows that the bigger the bore the more stopping power it delivers. Is that really true? Let's compare some basic black powder ballistics, then you make that decision.

The folks at Modern Muzzleloading spend a great deal of time at the shooting bench testing everything from new bullet and sabot designs, to the claims of certain lube makers, or even the longevity of a percussion nipple. They have also put thousands of rounds through their rifles to work up publishable ballistics for their .50 and .54 caliber in-line percussion rifles. In fact, they have two employees who do nothing but shoot from 8:00 a.m. to after 4:00 p.m. every day of the week.

What they have learned from all this shooting is that the .50-caliber is not only capable of matching the .54 for down-range energy, in many cases the half-inch bore will surpass the larger bore in actual killing energy. As noted earlier, the only loads which let the .54-caliber bore shine above the slightly smaller .50 is when a rifle is loaded with a patched round ball.

A 90-grain charge of Goex FFg black powder loaded behind a .490-inch round ball will produce right at 1,800 fps at the muzzle of a Knight rifle with 24-inch barrel. That load is also good for around 1,300 foot-pounds of energy. On the other hand, a 90-grain charge of Goex FFg loaded into a .54-caliber rifle will produce a muzzle velocity of about 1,750 fps. While the

• *With today's improved conical bullets, especially the effective saboted handgun bullets, the .50 will do anything the .54 can do...and usually do it better. Photo by Gary Clancy.*

heavier 230-grain round ball has a slightly slower muzzle velocity, it generates a greater muzzle energy of nearly 1,550 foot-pounds.

When the switch is made to shooting conical bullets, the roles begin to reverse somewhat. Modern Muzzleloading has found that a 100-grain charge of FFg or Pyrodex "RS" will produce an average muzzle velocity of about 1,400 fps when loaded behind one of the 385-grain, .50-caliber, conical Hornady Great Plains bullets. The energy generated by this load averages 1,675 foot-pounds.

The same 100-grain charge of powder loaded into a .54-caliber Knight rifle behind the same style bullet weighing 425 grains pushes the big conical bullet from the muzzle of the 24-inch barrel at about 1,300 fps. The bullet that is 40 grains heavier leaves the muzzle at nearly 100 fps slower than the same type of bullet out of a .50-caliber when pushed by an identical powder charge. Due to the slower velocity, the .54 rifle loaded with a Great Plains bullet actually produces about 80 foot-pounds less muzzle energy than the .50 when both are loaded with 100 grains of powder.

When shooting the saboted handgun bullets, there is no real difference in velocities or energy levels with the .50 and .54 caliber bores. The same range of bullet diameters and weights are available in both calibers. The only difference is the thickness of the plastic sabot used for each caliber bore.

For all practical purposes, Modern Muzzleloading has established that a 100 grain charge of powder (FFg and Pyrodex RS) will push any of the 260-grain jacketed .44- and .45-caliber handgun slugs from the muzzle of either a .50- or .54-caliber rifle at approximately 1,525 fps, with a muzzle energy of around 1,350 foot-pounds.

The old belief that a .54-caliber bore is better than the .50 in big game killing power is a myth dating from a time when early western hunters had only the patched round ball. With today's improved conical bullets, especially the effective saboted handgun bullets, the .50 will do anything the .54 can do...and usually do it better.

Of course, some readers will contend that you can stoke up the .54 to get more out of it, but the same holds true for the .50 caliber. **The fact is, with the .50-caliber**

Selecting a Deer Rifle

bore we have reached the point of diminishing return. To make a larger bore turn in better performance requires an investment in more powder and heavier lead. For this investment, the return usually is mostly greater recoil.

It's not my intention here to tell any of you which muzzleloader is best suited for your hunting. Only the individual who will be packing the frontloader can make that call. However, there have been several rifles which stick in my mind as favorites, mostly because the guns performed when the opportunity presented itself.

I bought my first muzzleloading rifle when I was 13 years old and hunted with the gun the next deer season. The rifle was one of 200 Belgian-made, .45-caliber percussion Kentucky rifles imported by Dixie Gun Works from 1956 until 1978. Back then I relied on a load that I wouldn't even begin to recommend today, just 70 grains of FFFg black powder and a patched 128-grain, .440-inch round ball.

This load is good for about 1,900 fps at the muzzle of the Dixie rifle's 40-inch barrel. The light 128-grain sphere of lead develops only about 1,100 foot-pounds of muzzle energy. By the time that ball reaches 100 yards, it hits home with only a little more than 300 foot-pounds of energy. A poor choice for whitetails, but at 14 years old I didn't know that.

I'll always remember opening morning of the 1963 Illinois deer season. Shortly after daybreak an old doe and a pair of fawns sauntered past my elevated tree stand. The deer were just 40 yards away and offered an easy shot. Does were legal, and I sure was tempted to take the larger of the three for my first muzzleloader kill. I also knew of several bucks using the same valley, so I let the deer pass.

The sun was just peeking over the horizon when I spotted a small eight-point buck approaching on the same trail the doe and fawns had used. As the deer came closer, my breathing became more and more difficult. I was a bundle of nerves by the time the buck stood 40 yards from my stand. Slowly, I brought the rifle up, held for the rear edge of the front shoulder and squeezed off the shot. That buck went just 50 yards before going down. I had my first

• *The author's first "serious" muzzleloading whitetail rifle was this customized version of the Thompson/Center Hawken built with a fast twist barrel for better accuracy with hard-hitting conical bullets.*

muzzleloader whitetail.

My first "serious" muzzleloading whitetail rifle was a .50 caliber Thompson/Center Hawken. I carried this rifle off and on for more than ten deer seasons, dropping more than a dozen whitetails with it.

Over the years I fired quite a few different loads through this rifle when shooting at paper, but when it came to shooting at whitetails there was only one load I would stuff into the frontloader. When I first started hunting with this rifle in 1973, I found 90 grains of FFg and one of Thompson/Center's big 370-grain Maxi-Ball conicals deadly on whitetails. The load is good for 1,480 fps and almost 1,800 foot-pounds of energy at the muzzle. At 100 yards, the big slug plows home with about 850 foot-pounds of energy. I took my first 100-yard-plus whitetail with this rifle and load.

If the big Thompson/Center slug has one fault, it's that it often punches right through a whitetail at close range before making a good transfer of energy. When I put together a new .50-caliber hunting rig to replace the Thompson/Center Hawken during the early 1980s, I also switched to a more effective bullet design.

The rifle started out as a project to build a true all-purpose muzzleloading rifle with interchangeable barrels for hunting both large and small game. The base for this rifle was one of the modern rifle stock designs Reinhart Fajen offers for replacing the traditionally styled stock of the Thompson/Center Hawken rifle. The stock accepts the barrel, lock, triggers and some of the other hardware found on the production frontloader.

For my all-purpose muzzleloader, I acquired a number of replacement "drop-in" barrels from Green Mountain Rifle Barrel Company in a variety of calibers ranging from .32 to .54. All were extremely accurate with the patched round ball, but the .50- and .54-caliber barrels offered by Green Mountain at that time were still rifled with slow twist for shooting the patched round ball. I was looking for a conical barrel and eventually settled on one of the factory Thompson/Center .50 caliber barrels.

Buffalo Bullet Company had just introduced their excellent swaged, hollow-point, lead Buffalo Maxi-Bullets. Once I replaced the rear sight on the Thompson/Center barrel with a Buehler base and rings and installed a Redfield 4X long-eye-relief scope, I was surprised to discover that I could print the heavy hunks of lead inside three inches at 100 yards. That rifle and bullet with 100 grains of FFg black powder cleanly dropped

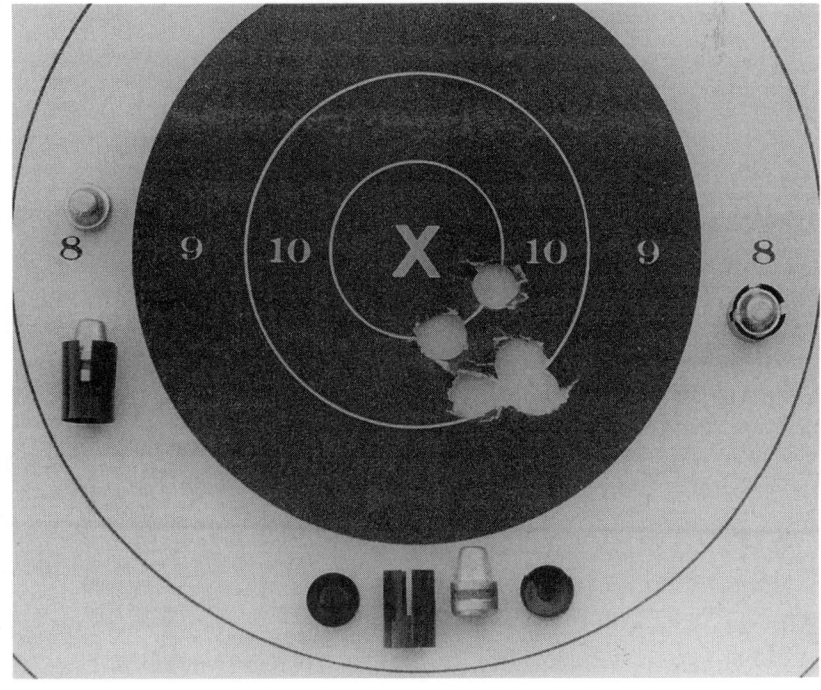

• The saboted handgun bullets are capable of delivering outstanding accuracy and performance on game. However, don't expect groups like this if your rifle has been built to shoot a patched round ball.

• *Whitetail buck following a doe through corn stubble during a late season hunt. The modern muzzleloading setups can reach out to 150 yards or more in situations like this. Photo by Richard P. Smith.*

a number of whitetails and other big game at ranges out to nearly 150 yards. The hollow-point design of the Buffalo Bullet did a better job of expanding at closer range than other heavy maxi-type bullets I'd shot up until then.

In the spring of 1986, I met William "Tony" Knight. He had been reading some of my articles in a number of outdoor and shooting magazines, most of which centered on my search for a serious muzzleloading big game rifle. He and I shared a number of thoughts on what it would take to build the ultimate muzzleloading deer rifle, but Tony took it a step or two farther.

His first rifles featured a one-turn-in-48 inches rate of rifling twist, which then was considered fast for a muzzleloader. I'd been playing around with several custom cut barrels with rates of twist as fast as a turn in 24 inches, and my findings were enough to encourage Tony to experiment with various fast rates of rifling twist. In short order, he made a switch to one-turn-in-32 inches as the standard rate of twist in the in-line rifles he was then building on special order in a small workshop in his garage.

In 1988, Modern Muzzleloading made another change in the rate of rifling twist in their barrels, moving to an even faster one-turn-in-28 inches. Through thousands and thousands of rounds, Tony and several other shooters in his company had determined that the slightly faster rate of twist better handled a wider range of conical hunting bullets, especially the saboted handgun bullets. The accuracy of the Knight rifle is now legendary, and when you take the time to work up your loads you will find this rifle is capable of printing 1-1/2 inch groups at 100 yards. Since meeting Tony back when Modern Muzzleloading was a two-man operation in his garage, the Knight rifle has remained my personal choice for all big game hunting. I shoot several different stainless .50 caliber models and have taken more than 30 whitetails with the rifles, never having to shoot one twice.

These have been just a few of my favorite muzzleloading hunting rifles in the more than 30 years I've hunted with a rifle of frontloading design. I've found the challenge of hunting with a muzzleloader to fall somewhere between bowhunting and using a modern firearm. Whichever model you choose, work to develop the most effective load the rifle will shoot accurately. Then spend a great deal of time shooting the muzzleloader. Proven accuracy on target paper builds confidence in the deer woods.

The challenge is knowing that you have only a one-shot chance to down the game cleanly, and making that shot count. It is a most satisfying way to take your deer.

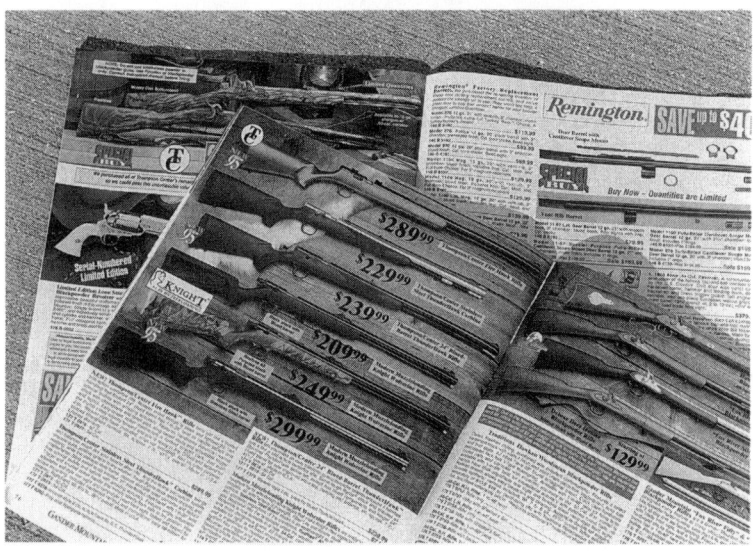

● *More and more retail stores have good black powder departments, of rifles and accessories, so you can get hands-on inspection and personal advice to get the best rifle and gear for your needs and preferences. Catalogs also have good selections.*

Selecting a Deer Rifle

• The accessories rack at any black powder store or department usually has a wide range of items. It's up to you to decide which you need and which would just be nice to have.

• Barnes Expander MZ, one of the many new bullets designed specifically for muzzleloaders.

Chapter 5

Accessories Or Necessities?

Muzzleloading is one of those sports which can be approached in two different manners. The first is to "get by" with the absolute minimum amount of equipment necessary. The other route, the "luxury" route, is to own practically every gadget and gizmo introduced!

There are a number of so-called accessories that are so important to the muzzleloading deer hunter they should be considered necessities. While the number of so-called accessories available to today's black powder shooter almost is overwhelming, the serious hunter usually will find that the fewer carried into the woods, the more enjoyable and often more successful the hunt. Keeping things simple and less cluttered is the best advice I can give someone looking at muzzleloading for the first time.

One of the most important accessories the black powder hunter can own is a good container for packing powder into the field. Through the ages, shooters and hunters have relied on a wide range of horns and flasks for doing just that. One of the best available today is a sturdy cylindrical flask which will accommodate about a third of a pound of black powder or Pyrodex. A number of suppliers currently offer a flask of this design, and a few even offer it with a choice of powder dispensing spouts.

Connecticut Valley Arms markets three variations. One relies on a plunger arrangement which drops approximately 20 grains of powder when depressed. Another relies on the old-fashioned lever and gate arrangement, just like most revolver powder flasks dating from the mid-1800s. The best arrangement for today's hunter is CVA's cylindrical flask with a spring-loaded valve. The flask is reasonably weather tight, and the thumb operated valve remains open to fill a measure as long as it's depressed. Spring pressure automatically cuts off the powder flow the instant the pressure is removed.

Experienced black powder burners know that a shooter should never dump a powder charge into the muzzle directly from the powder flask or horn. Yet, several accessory suppliers market flasks and horns with interchangeable spouts for exact powder charges, encouraging this dangerous practice. Modern Muzzleloading now offers a flask and measure as a matched set. This arrangement, however, requires that the separate measure be totally removed from the flask before the powder charge can be

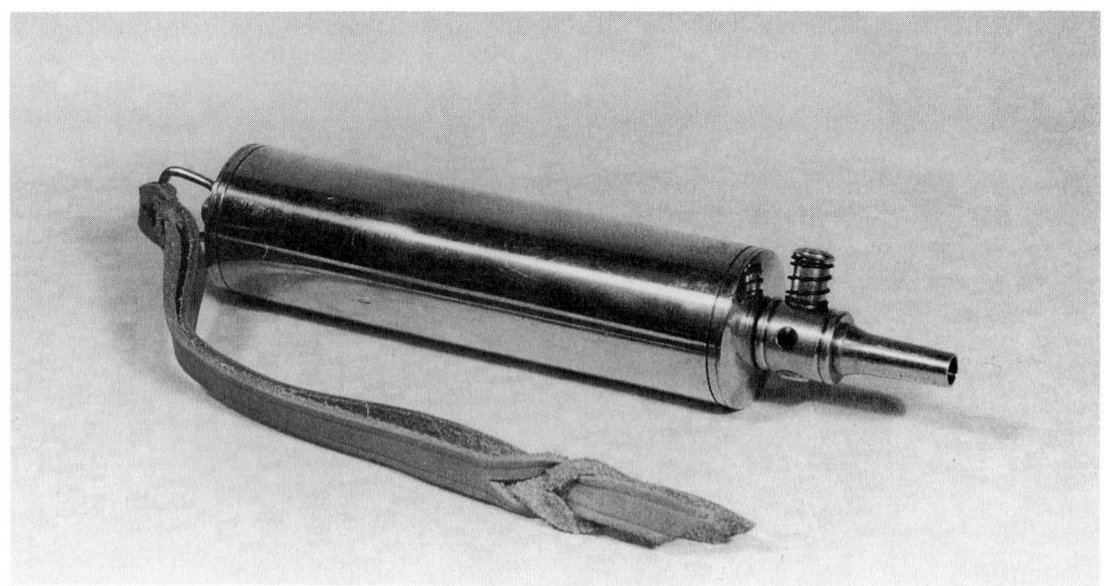

• Cylindrical powder flasks such as this are sturdy, well built and are the author's choice for dispensing powder charges for a muzzleloading rifle.

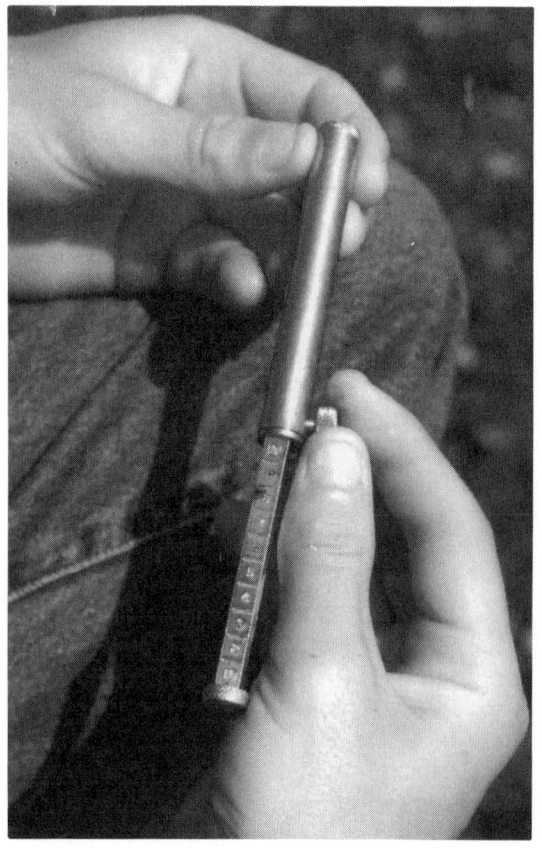

• A quality adjustable measure is an absolute must for the muzzleloading hunter who demands consistent accuracy from his frontloading hunting rifle.

poured into the barrel. A spring loaded cut-off valve automatically levels the powder charge, eliminating a waste of powder. The measure can be adjusted to drop charges from 10 to 120 grains.

The powder measure is one of the most important accessories a black powder shooter can own. Top performance from any frontloading gun, whether it's a rifle, pistol, revolver, musket or scattergun, depends on consistent powder charges. While most of the measures commercially available are of the adjustable type, graduated in five- and/or ten-grain increments, such a measure isn't all that necessary. Any type of measure, even a cut off centerfire cartridge case or hollowed-out wooden tube or section of deer antler, will allow you to make sure your frontloader is loaded with the same amount of powder for every shot.

One of the adjustable measures is nice if you use different powder charges for different ranges, like to experiment with loads or shoot more than one black powder gun. Navy Arms produces a handy adjustable measure with settings from 10 to 120 grains, marked in ten-grain increments. Any setting can be locked into place by tightening a knurled nut on the side of the measure, insuring that charges will remain the same until you purposely change the setting. A funnel top swivels to one side for easy filling of the measure, then swivels back over the tip of the measure to level the powder charge and provide a pour spout that will get every granule of powder into the bore. The bottom of this measure unscrews to reveal a stiff, small diameter wire that works well as a nipple or vent pick.

Thompson/Center Arms also produces a well-built, adjustable brass powder measure. This one is adjustable from 20 to 120 grains, with a locking, knurled collet keeping the measure at the desired setting until you are ready to switch to a different powder charge. Instead of a swiveling funnel head, the Thompson/Center measure features a head that slips back and forth. To fill the measure, the funnel is pushed to the side, out of the way. The measure is then filled and the funnel pushed back over the powder charge. The powder charge is automatically leveled and the funnel allows easy pouring of the charge into the muzzle of the gun. The base of this measure is a compartment for caps, holding about 20 standard No. 11 percussion caps.

Another important accessory is the ball starter, especially when bulk patching material is being used. Most starters are fashioned with a short 1/4-inch section of rod and a longer four- to six-inch section of rod. The body of the starter can be a wooden ball, a heavy piece of deer antler or even a modern polyurethane casting resin.

When using the ball starter with bulk patching material, the ball and cloth are pressed into the bore as far as they will go with thumb pressure. Next, the short 1/4-inch section of rod is used to get the ball and patch slightly below the crown of the muzzle. This is done simply by smacking the backside of the starter with the palm of the hand. Once the ball and cloth patch are into the bore, a patch knife can be used to trim away excess material flush with the muzzle. The longer rod of the starter is then used to push the patched round ball further into the bore to allow room for the insertion of the ramrod, which is used to seat the ball over the powder charge.

When using pre-cut patches, it gener-

● *This flask and powder measure arrangement requires that the measured charge be separated from the flask of powder before it is dumped into the muzzle of the rifle. This is a safe practice all black powder shooters need to adopt.*

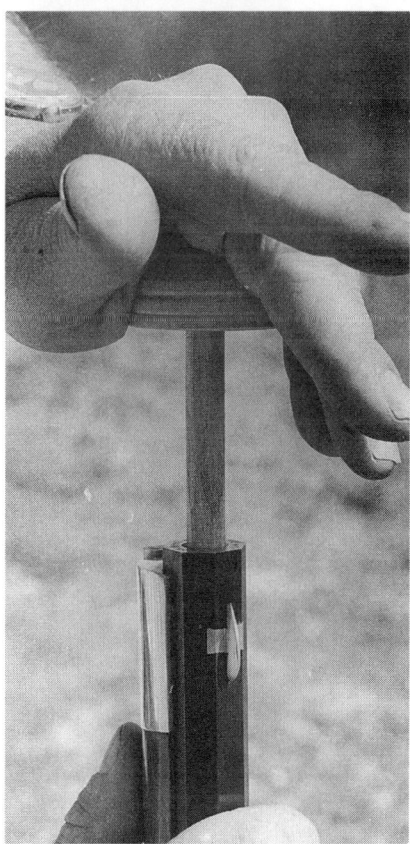

● *A short or ball starter makes it easy to start a projectile into the bore of a frontloading rifle. Once the ball or bullet is pushed several inches into the bore, the ramrod is used to seat it over the powder.*

Accessories/Necessities

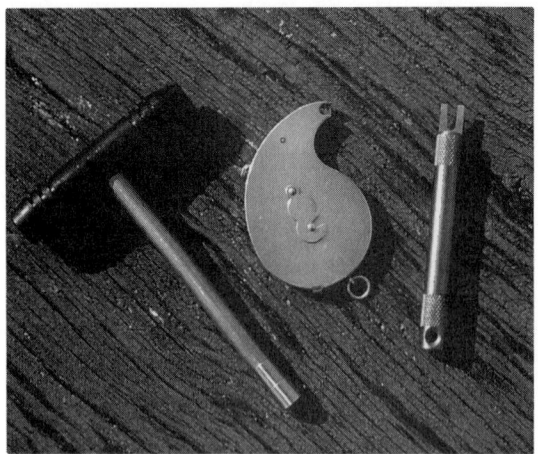

• The Knight M-P Bullet Starter, universal in-line capper and decapper shown here make loading and shooting the in-line percussion rifles a lot less tedious.

• A capper is a necessity when using an in-line rifle, because there just isn't enough room for your fingers. Photo by Gary Clancy.

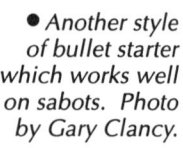

• Another style of bullet starter which works well on sabots. Photo by Gary Clancy.

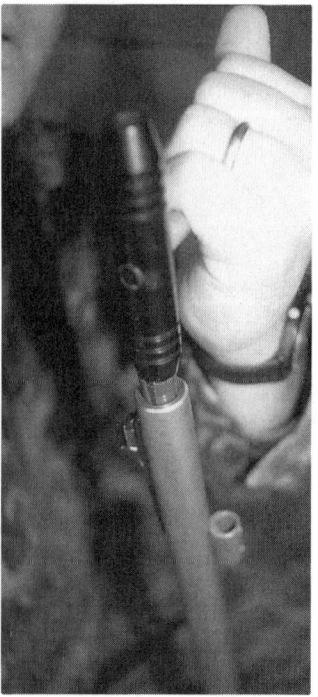

ally isn't necessary to use the short section of the starter. Instead, the ball is centered in the patch, with the patch centered over the bore. The long section of rod is then placed atop the ball and the patch and ball are pushed into the bore with a healthy shove on the top of the starter.

Some of the elongated conical bullets rely on oversized bearing bands for a precise fit with the bore. To get the rifling to engrave these bands often requires a considerable amount of pressure on the bullet nose. The use of a short starter helps to get these bullets started by pushing them into the bore four or five inches, at which point the rifling has fully engraved any oversized portions of the bullet.

Most mail-order muzzleloading suppliers sell a short starter or ball starter. Most are simply a 1-1/2- to two-inch diameter wooden ball with two rod sections set into it. A hardwood dowel is commonly used for these rods, but occasionally brass or a special nonabrasive plastic is used. Some competition shooters rely on a short steel starter with a nylon bushing that protects the rifling at the muzzle from wear.

Another handy accessory from Modern Muzzleloading is their new Knight M-P Bullet Starter. The M-P stands for multi-purpose, and that's the best way to describe this arrangement. Just as the name suggests, the tool is a bullet starter. However, it also is a cleaning extension for the Knight rifle aluminum ramrod, a palm saver when loading and shooting at the range, plus an assist handle which can quickly and easily be slipped over the end of the ramrod to help seat tight fitting projectiles.

Percussion rifle hunters will quickly realize the value of a good capper, especially when trying to reload for a fast second shot. Fishing out a single cap from a full tin of a hundred with your fingertips, then getting it in place on the nipple, can prove to be a real pain. The colder the weather, the more difficult it becomes.

Easily the best capper available today is one produced by Tedd Cash of Cash Manufacturing. Tedd's capper is a dead ringer for a high quality original built in the mid-1800s. The oval arrangement will hold

75 No. 11 percussion caps and is one of the easiest to load. The lid hinges upward, and the caps pour right in. As many of the caps will be lying on their side as right side up. However, to get all the caps sitting cup-up just shake the capper lightly. Being heavier on the closed end, the caps turn right over and, in a few seconds, they're all sitting the way they should.

This is one of the most trouble-free cappers available. A thumb operated button on the side feeds a single cap to where it can be positioned on the nipple. This capper is solidly built. You don't have to worry about bending it if it happens to be in your back pocket when you sit down.

This capper is offered in two styles, an oval shaped design for traditionally styled side-hammer rifles and a teardrop shape for percussion revolvers and in-line percussion rifles.

Powder flask, measure, capper and short starter, along with a pocketful of bullets, and you are ready for a day in the deer woods. Many whitetail hunters are now packing "quick load tubes" to reduce the amount of loose components in the pockets of their hunting jackets. These tubes feature a removable cap on each end, allowing you to carry a pre-measured powder charge and projectile in the tube ready to be loaded into the rifle. To use, all you have to do is remove the cap from the powder end of the tube, pour it in, then remove the cap from the projectile end and, using either a short starter or the ramrod itself, shove the projectile on through the tube and into the bore.

It's important that tubes of the proper caliber are used. To prevent powder from getting around to the front of the bullet, the projectile must fit snugly inside the tube. For instance, if a .54-caliber loading tube is used to carry loads for a .50-caliber rifle, the ball or bullet will fit so loosely that powder can filter past the bullet and end up on the wrong side. The result can be inconsistent amounts of powder behind the projectile, which can and often will affect accuracy, or a projective which is "dirty" from powder which has found its way to the front side. With a lubed "maxi" style conical bullet, powder granules

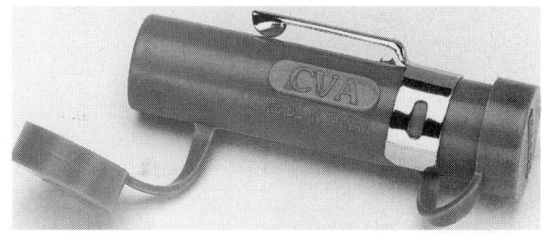

• Quick-load tubes like this from Connecticut Valley Arms let the black powder hunter handily carry powder and bullet in one unit to make reloading in the field much easier.

• Powder flask, measure, capper and short starter, along with a pocketful of bullets, and you are ready for a day in the deer woods. Photo by Gary Clancy.

Accessories/Necessities

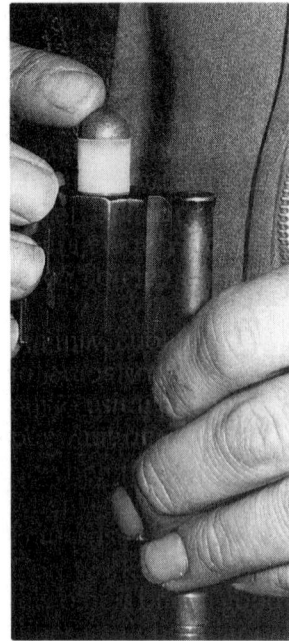
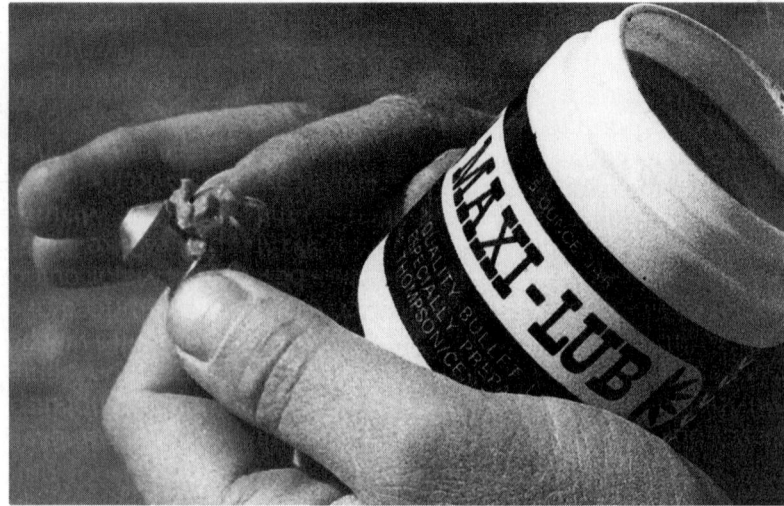
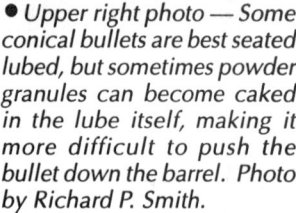
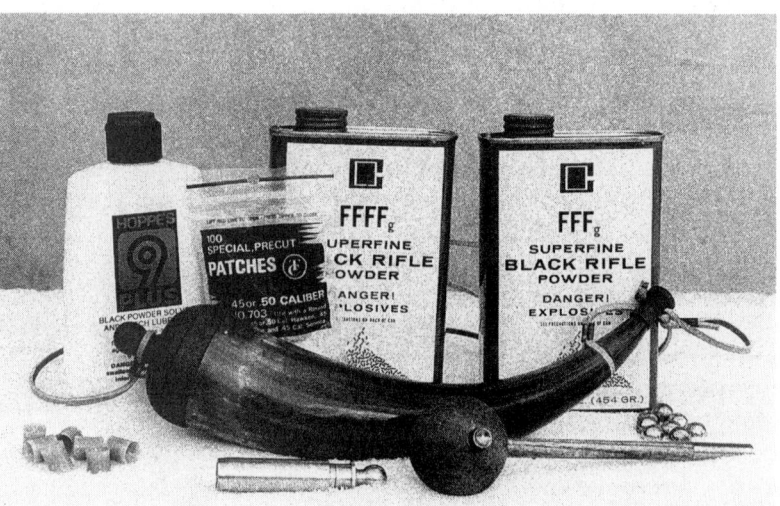

- *Upper right photo — Some conical bullets are best seated lubed, but sometimes powder granules can become caked in the lube itself, making it more difficult to push the bullet down the barrel. Photo by Richard P. Smith.*
- *Poly patches can be an easier, more consistent system than cloth patches for round ball shooting. Photo above by Richard P. Smith.*
- *The necessities for a ball gun, right. Photo by Tom Fegely.*

can become caked in the lube itself. Once powder finds its way around the bullet, it often becomes more difficult to push the bullet from the tube, into the bore and down the barrel.

When a loading tube of the proper caliber is used, it can cut reloading time practically in half. When both powder and projectile can be carried handily inside a single loader, it eliminates fumbling for a powder flask, measure and loose bullet when a quick reload is needed. Butler Creek Enterprises, Thompson/Center Arms, Dixie Gun works, Modern Muzzleloading and a few others offer a good variety of quick-load tubes in all popular calibers.

Connecticut Valley Arms refers to their "4-In-1" T-Loader as the ultimate preloader. It is the handiest quick-load tube I have ever hunted with. The 4-In-1 T-Loader, just as the name implies, serves four functions. Since it is made of clear Lexan plastic, you can tell at a glance whether or not the loader is loaded. Best of all, by being able to see through the loader, you can rely on the graduated powder scale right on the tube to measure powder charges. The tube is also molded with a handy ball starter and a recess which slips over the end of the ramrod to aid in seating a tight-fitting projectile. This handy little accessory is a preloader with separate compartments for powder and bul-

• We don't like to anthropomorphize, but the temptation was too great here in combination with the photo at left. Candidates for this deer caption are: 1) "Did I hear a noise?" 2) "125 yards? Nah, it's at least 165." Photo by Gary Clancy.

• Shooting practice under "real" conditions can pay dividends during hunting season. Photo by Betty Lou Fegely.

• The best way to learn what are necessities and what are not – and to get to know your rifle – is simple: do a lot of shooting. It's all part of that old statement – the harder and smarter you work (or scout and hunt), the luckier you get. Photo by Tom Fegely.

Accessories/Necessities

let, a powder measure, a ball starter and a palm saver all wrapped in one.

Once you have acquired the basic accessories which make loading easier and more convenient, not to mention more consistent, you can shop around for those other luxury items which make the sport a little more pleasant. These include a small knapping hammer for keeping the striking edge of a flint on a flintlock sharp, a nipple wrench for the percussion guns, a loading block for faster reloading in the field, a patch cutter for producing pre-cut patches at home, a traditionally styled powder horn, a leather hunting bag, a screw-in funnel for spill-free filling of a powder flask, a specially adapted nipple and cover that makes a percussion hunting rifle virtually waterproof, a set of sling swivels or a slip-on sling, a mechanical starter for the Maxi-Ball, one of the stainless steel combination loading/cleaning rods, or perhaps even a shooting box to carry some of these items out to the range or to deer camp.

When working up loads and shooting for optimum accuracy, there are a wide range of accessories which can make an afternoon out more rewarding. However, when it's time to head for the deer woods, the simpler you can keep things the better. Those accessories described here are the necessities for today's black powder hunter. Anything else you carry is sure to get in the way and weight you down.

Chapter 6

Working Up Hunting Loads

Today's muzzleloading hunter basically has three choices when selecting a bullet for hunting big game:
1) the patched round ball,
2) a heavy pure lead conical bullet,
3) a saboted modern pistol bullet.

Of the three, the patched round ball is the least effective. Being a perfect sphere, the round ball loses velocity quickly, and along with speed it also sheds much needed downrange energy.

The heavy pure lead conical bullets, weighing up to twice as much as a patched round ball for the same caliber rifle, do a great job of maintaining high energy levels out to and past 100 yards. However, because of their tremendous weight, these bullets are notorious for excessive drop past the hundred-yard mark.

The best of both worlds can be achieved by shooting the saboted handgun bullets out of a muzzleloading big game rifle. The system allows a shooter to load and hunt with several hundred different .44- and .45-caliber jacketed and non-jacketed handgun bullets out of a .50- or .54-caliber muzzleloader. With bullet weights ranging from as light as 180 grains to more than 400 grains, the small plastic sabots allow you to better tailor loads to the specific game being hunted.

This chapter will take a look at the different types of projectiles available to today's muzzleloading big game hunter and how to approach working up effective hunting loads.

Most whitetails, the number one target of today's black powder big game hunter, are taken at less than 50 yards. In most rifles legal for hunting whitetails, the patched round ball ahead of powder charges of 70 to 98 grains of FFg or FFFg will definitely develop enough killing energy to drop even the biggest buck at such ranges, especially when the hunter has the forethought to go after this fine game animal with a rifle of .50 or .54 caliber.

A 178-grain, .490-inch round ball pushed out of the muzzle of a 28-inch barreled Hawken reproduction by an 80-grain charge of FFg exits the bore at approximately 1,800 fps (Thompson/Center ballistics). At the muzzle, this load develops over 1,300 foot-pounds of energy (Thompson/Center ballistics) and by the time the sphere of lead has traveled 30 or even 50 yards, it hasn't slowed much and the ballistics have not changed all that drastically.

Loads

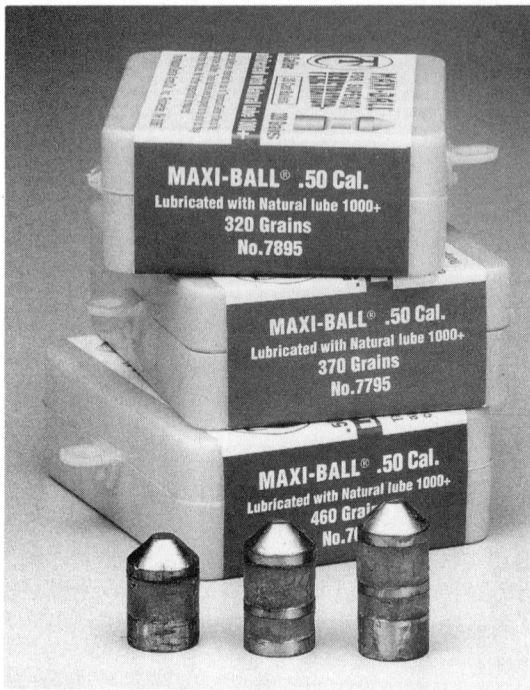

- The round ball is a poor performer on deer beyond 75 yards but does an acceptable job at close range. The flattened discs are .490" balls recovered from whitetails taken at ranges of 20 to 30 yards.

- Conical bullets like the Thompson/Center Maxi-Ball retain energy at extended ranges better than does a patched round ball.

- The hollow-pointed Buffalo Bullet conicals expand well on deer-sized game. Mushroomed bullet was recovered from a big whitetail buck dropped at just over one hundred yards.

• When you know your rifle's limits and stay within them, things tend to work out. This is frontier re-creation — coonskin cap, buckskins, homemade flintlock. Photo by Tom Fegeley.

• Conical hunting bullets have been in use since the early 1800s. Many fine originals, such as this percussion double, were built to shoot heavy elongated hunting bullets.

Loads

• *Before attempting to load and shoot a brand new muzzleloader, first take the time to read the owner's manual and to familiarize yourself with features of the new gun.*

A soft, pure lead round ball driven home behind the shoulder of a good-sized whitetail buck at such short range with upward of 1,000 foot-pounds of energy does so with quite a wallop. The ball is generally flattened into a lead disc half again the diameter of the ball's original size. About as often as not, the ball fails to penetrate completely through the animal and the transfer of energy is complete. The result is usually a clean kill, provided the hunter has hit his mark.

What about those shots closer to 100 yards with the patched round ball? The same ball that was pushed from the muzzle of a .50-caliber Hawken at 1,800 fps has slowed to the point at 100 yards that it strikes the target with about only 400 pounds of remaining energy, roughly half as much as the obsolete old .25/35 Winchester round.

Hardly a potent deer killer! Yet, quite a few muzzleloading hunters going afield each fall rely on such loads, and in a few states it's even illegal to use anything but a patched round ball during the special muzzleloading big game hunts or seasons.

As more and more modern hunters turn to muzzleloaders to cash in on the additional bonus hunting provided by the special black powder seasons, there is a growing concern with improving the effectiveness of the old-fashioned rifles on larger game. Today's hunter is trying to make his frontloader perform more like the modern centerfire guns he's accustomed to carrying afield, and there's presently a good selection of hard-hitting conical bullets available that increase the chances of taking big game out to and past distances that have always perplexed patched round ball shooters.

Actually, conical bullets are far from being a novel idea. During the early 1800s, there were all sorts of attempts to develop the "perfect" muzzleloading rifle bullet. As early as 1830 some U.S. riflemen were experimenting with what is often referred to as the "sugarloaf" or "picket" bullet -- a conical shape sort of like an acorn. At about the same time, gunmakers and shooters in England and throughout continental Europe were also working hard to produce a "modern" projectile for the muzzleloading rifle, something more effective than the round ball and easier to load.

Had the likes of Warren Center of Thompson/Center Arms, Richard Lee of Lee Precision, and Ron Dahlitz of Buffalo Bullet Company been around during the early 1800s, conical muzzleloading bullets would surely have seen much wider use. Then, perhaps, today's shooters wouldn't be arguing so much over what's traditional and what's not!

When Warren Center sat down and designed his now widely used Thompson/Center Hawken rifle, which appeared on the market in 1970, he designed right along with the rifle a conical bullet especially for today's muzzleloading big game hunter. That bullet was the now popular Maxi-Ball. Center's solid conical bullet design marked the first real improvement in projectiles for the muzzleloading rifle since the Minie design of the 1860s.

These elongated slugs are approximately twice as long as in diameter, and likewise approximately double the weight of the round ball fired in the same caliber rifle. Thompson/Center's big .54-caliber Maxi weighs a whopping 430 grains; the popular .50-caliber slug tips the scales at 370 grains; while the .45-caliber version still weighs a healthy 240 grains to turn even this borderline whitetail rifle into potent medicine for deer and other big game. (Note, the .45-caliber Maxi is more than 60 grains heavier than the round ball for .50-caliber rifle!)

The Maxi-Ball solid conical bullet design was a big improvement, and it could be loaded without a patch.

Another factor adding to the popularity of the Maxi is the fact that these bullets are loaded without any sort of patching. The design relies on a slightly undersized base and middle bearing band, then another band near the nose of the bullet that's several thousandths of an inch oversized. To load, a lubed bullet is simply pushed into the muzzle until the oversized forward bearing band makes contact with the lands of the rifling. The undersized base and middle bands ideally ride right on top of the lands without offering any resistance whatsoever. Using a short starter, the bullet is then pushed on into the bore with a few pounds of pressure on the nose of the slug. The soft lead band is easily engraved by the rifling, and once the bullet is pushed into the bore of the rifle with the short starter, it is easily

Loads

seated over the powder charge with little, if any, resistance.

Bullet obturation, or flattening of the projectile in the bore at the moment of ignition, forces the two undersized bearing bands into the bottoms of the grooves, forming the necessary gas seal and a precise fit of the bullet with the rifle's bore. The shallower the grooves, the easier the seal is made, and Thompson/Center, along with a large number of other manufacturers today, relies on button rifling of only about .005- to .006-inch depth, well suited for the Maxi-type bullet. Also, since the length of these bullets are nearly twice their diameter, Thompson/Center and many of today's other manufacturers/importers rifle the bores with a relatively fast one-turn-in-48 inches rate of twist. This fast twist imparts sufficient spin on the big bullets to insure accuracy and to prevent keyholing.

There are several good conicals available, but the saboted pistol bullet is a whole new world.

The ready acceptance of the Maxi-Ball as an alternative to the often ineffective patched round ball has led to the development of several other easy-loading, hard-hitting conical bullets. One of the first to follow the Thompson/Center design was the R.E.A.L. (Rifling Engraved At Loading) bullet from Lee Precision. Richard Lee's design incorporates not one but up to four oversized bearing bands that must be engraved by the rifling as the bullet is loaded into the muzzle. These bands are only about .001-inch larger in diameter than true bore size and offer very little resistance when poked through the muzzle with a short starter. A tapered edge around the base makes loading this bullet reasonably easy, and the bullet is automatically centered in the bore. Lee's precision molds for producing the R.E.A.L. bullets are available in .44, .45, .50, .54, and .58 caliber, with two different weights and lengths for each.

While conicals such as the Thompson/Center Maxi-Ball and Lee Precision R.E.A.L. bullet will retain much needed energy for those lengthy shots at big game, they also have a bad tendency to punch right through close-range targets without a good transfer of energy. Generally speaking, as long as you are able to put the heavy conicals through the vitals of a big game animal just 30 or 40 yards away, the target will go down. However, it also is possible that you will be faced with a lengthy tracking job when one of the bullets passes through without transferring sufficient energy for a clean kill.

One design which helps to remedy this problem is the hollow-pointed Maxi Bullets from the Buffalo Bullet Company. Unlike the two conical designs already discussed, there are no molds for casting these bullets. Even the company that produces the Buffalo Bullets doesn't rely on molds, but instead swages the bullets from cold, pure lead, relying on heavy duty hydraulic presses and precision dies. The result is a bullet completely free of mould seams and sprue marks, available in .45, .50, and .54 caliber, with both a hollow-based and solid-based version for each caliber. All come pre-lubed, 20 to the box.

Also, unlike the other two designs already discussed, Buffalo Bullets do not feature any oversized bearing bands whatsoever. Instead, the cylindrical sides of the bullet feature a heavily knurled surface that forms a snug fit with the lands of the rifling. Even so, in most bores these bullets can be started with nothing more than thumb pressure. The solid-based design relies entirely on bullet obturation for a precision fit with the grooves of the rifling, while the hollow-based version relies on both obturation and expansion of the hollow base into the rifling.

The hollow point of the Buffalo Bullet conicals does an excellent job of expansion at practically all ranges. Hunters who have shot deer at short 30 and 40 yard ranges report that the big bullet still commonly pokes all the way through the target, but from the ever enlarging wound channel it's evident that there's a great deal of energy

• *Good loads will be consistently accurate and hard hitting at distances longer than you'll want to shoot with just the naked eye. This big Saskatchewan whitetail fell to Richard Smith's well-rigged black powder outfit. Photo by Richard P. Smith.*

transfer. On targets out to and past 100 yards, recovered bullets display picture perfect, rolled back expansion. It's not uncommon for .45-caliber Maxi Bullets to expand well past .60 caliber, .50-caliber slugs to increase to over .80 caliber and the big .54-caliber slugs to roll back and flatten to nearly .90 caliber. Few hunters report anything running off once it has been struck by one of the hollow-pointed Buffalo Bullets!

A new and very modern approach to giving the old fashioned muzzleloaders something of a ballistic face lift are the unique plastic sabots now being manufactured by Muzzleload Magnum Products, Modern Muzzleloading, Thompson/Center and a few others. These allow you to load and shoot either jacketed or cast pistol slugs for modern center-fire handguns in larger bore muzzleloading rifles.

Shooters who have tried the new loading system have reported exceptional accuracy from the saboted handgun bullets when shot in rifles having relatively shallow button rifled grooves with a twist in the neighborhood of one-turn-in-48 inches. Tony

Knight has done considerable testing with the sabots in his in-line muzzleloading rifles. These frontloaders are rifled with an exceptionally fast one-turn-in-28 inches twist, especially designed to produce best performance with a conical bullet. The inventor of this rifle recommends shooting sabots in his rifles over anything else on the market. His favorite load for a .50-caliber rifle that he's used to down a number of deer and black bear is 110 grains of Pyrodex RS behind a Modern Muzzleloading 310-grain lead hollow point of .45 caliber. This load of powder pushes the bullet from the muzzle of the 24-inch barreled rifle at velocities over 1,600 fps.

> *The introduction of Pyrodex did as much for black powder shooting as did any given rifle.*

When shooting the saboted handgun bullets, there is no real difference in velocities or energy levels with the .50- and .54-caliber bores. The same range of bullet diameters and weights are available to shooters of both calibers. The only difference is the thickness of the plastic sabot used for each caliber bore.

For all practical purposes, Modern Muzzleloading has established that a 100-grain charge of powder (FFg and Pyrodex RS) will push any of the 260-grain jacketed .44- or .45-caliber handgun slugs from the muzzle of either a .50- or .54-caliber rifle at approximately 1600 fps, with a muzzle energy of around 1,350 foot-pounds.

Since switching to shooting and hunting with saboted handgun bullets for big game nearly eight years ago, I have come to a number of conclusions. First, I feel that **saboted handgun bullets are superior to all other projectiles** for the muzzleloading big game rifle. While today's shooter has the convenience of buying sabots and bullets already matched for his rifle's bore, he also can purchase the sabots by themselves and select from more than 200 bullet weights, types and manufacture.

The sabot system lets you tailor a load for the species of game being hunted. One thing is certain, you don't need the same bullet for hunting pronghorns as you would use on something as big as a moose.

For years, several of the larger manufacturers and importers of muzzleloading guns claimed that the warranty on their rifles was void if the owner shot a plastic sabot or patching out of their guns. Today, they market saboted bullets of their own. It is simply the most efficient projectile system for the muzzleloading hunting rifle, and hunters across the country are making the switch from traditional patched round balls and conical lead bullets. (Unfortunately, there still are a few states which deny the black powder hunter an opportunity to hunt big game with a truly effective hunting projectile.)

I have personally fired more than 5,000 saboted rounds out of .50- and .54-caliber rifles. From this experience and from talking with other shooters who have fired a large number of rounds with sabots, I also have come to the conclusion that **the closer the bullet is to bore size, the better the accuracy.** This simply means shooting the .45 caliber instead of .44-caliber handgun slugs in either the .50 or .54.

The less plastic between bullet and bore, the better. For that reason, most .50-caliber rifles will turn in better accuracy than .54-caliber rifles when loaded with saboted handgun bullets.

The introduction of Pyrodex in the mid 1970s did as much for black powder shooting as the introduction of any given muzzleloading rifle. The powder was then -- and remains -- the only successful substitute for black powder ever to be marketed.

So, if both can be loaded and shot in a muzzleloading gun, what's the real difference between the two?

What really sets Pyrodex apart from its ancient counterpart is that it is a flammable solid, while black powder is classified as a Class A explosive. Pyrodex is actually a smokeless powder which has been specially

• The ready availability of Pyrodex has made it the most widely used powder in today's frontloading guns.

formulated to produce the lower pressures of black powder, making it safe to load and shoot in a firearm of frontloading design.

The fact that Pyrodex is not a Class A explosive allows gun shops to stock the powder without all the red tape and insurance problems generally associated with black powder. The ready availability of Pyrodex has made it the most widely used powder in today's frontloading guns. Although the majority of deer hunters who head for the woods with their favorite smokepole now do so with it stoked with a load of Pyrodex, many still question whether their rifle would perform better with black powder. It's doubtful.

The .50-caliber in-line rifle I use for the majority of my big game hunting turns in the tightest groups when loaded with a charge of FFg black powder behind a saboted, 260-grain, .45-caliber, jacketed hollow-pointed pistol bullet. When all things are right, including the shooter, I am able to consistently print groups of 1-1/2 inches at 100 yards.

About the best I can expect from a load of Pyrodex RS behind the same bullet are groups closer to two inches across. The difference is insignificant, especially when shooting at a target the size of a whitetail buck.

Pyrodex does, however, offer other advantages over black powder, making it my powder choice for all my hunts each fall. The most significant of these favorable properties is that Pyrodex doesn't tend

Loads

• *For best accuracy, always run a patch dampened with saliva or a cleaning solution down the bore between each shot to keep fouling from building up.*

to foul the barrel as heavily as black powder, nor does the fouling tend to build with each succeeding shot.

Fouling is a factor which really can destroy accuracy, and one which you easily can learn to deal with. Unfortunately, a large number of the hunters toting a muzzleloader into the deer woods settle for just so-so accuracy when they could enjoy much better groups at 50, 75 or even 100 yards simply by taking a few seconds to wipe fouling from the bore after each shot.

Black powder is a mixture of saltpeter (potassium nitrate), sulphur and charcoal. The basic formula for the propellant hasn't changed in more than 700 years. The fact tht black powder burns exceptionally dirty and is highly corrosive hasn't changed in all that time either.

The fouling left from a single shot of black powder is heavy enough to make it all but impossible to load a second shot, and in most rifles the thought of loading a third shot without taking time to wipe the bore free of fouling is just a dream. Plus, this build-up of fouling results in a steady rise in internal pressures, which affect accuracy.

While the fouling from a single shot of Pyrodex can be nearly as corrosive as shooting black powder, making a thorough cleaning of any muzzleloader necessary at the end of the day, the fact that fouling doesn't continue to build with each shot makes for easier loading of follow-up shots in the deer woods. **In fact, I've loaded upward of 20 shots with Pyrodex without taking time to wipe the bore.** However, when shooting for accuracy, especially when working up a new hunting load for a rifle, I'll always wipe the bore between shots, even with Pyrodex. Wiping the bore with a damp patch between each shot pays off.

In a hurried situation, the ability to reload the rifle quickly could make a real difference between hanging your tag on a whitetail or possibly losing it. Accuracy with Pyrodex loads can be affected by fouling build up, but not so much as to destroy hunting accuracy. My rifle keeps five-shot groups around two inches when I take the time to wipe Pyrodex fouling from the bore between each shot. The same five shots fired through the same bore, without wiping the fouling between shots, usually results in groups which open to three to 3-1/2 inches at 100 yards. Again, the slight trade-off in accuracy is a bargain for the benefit of being able to reload the rifle quickly.

With 100 grains of FFg black powder, my .50-caliber in-line rifle pushes a saboted, 260-grain, jacketed hollow-point, .45-caliber pistol bullet from the muzzle of the 24-inch barrel at about 1,600 fps. The load generates almost 1,400 foot pounds of energy at the muzzle.

A switch to 100 grains of Pyrodex RS increases muzzle velocity to 1,650 fps and pushes muzzle energy to about 1,450 foot-pounds. While this represents little difference in the performance of either load on whitetails out to 150 yards, the Pyrodex load is superior ballistically to the black powder load.

In several states, the muzzleloading deer hunter still cannot load and hunt with a saboted pistol bullet, so must choose between a patched round ball or heavy lead conical bullet. Many experienced black powder shooters have discovered that, while Pyrodex may perform just as well as black powder behind a patched round ball, the powder simply tends to fall a little short in the accuracy department when loaded behind one of the maxi-style conical bullets.

For the most part, my findings concur. Just about every time I tried to work up loads for heavy conical bullets using Pyrodex, I found FFg black powder turned in much better accuracy. That is, until I started experimenting with the coarser CTG grade of Pyrodex in the in-line percussion rifles.

Several years ago, I did quite a bit of loading for an original black powder cartridge model Sharp rifle with Pyrodex CTG. When I tried to load the coarser grained powder in traditional side-hammer muzzleloaders, I found the ignition less than great. When the hammer fell, the powder charge stuffed down the barrel was just as likely to ignite as it was to fire. The coarser powder was simply hard to ignite with the spark of a percussion cap in traditionally styled muzzleloaders. The design of these rifles wastes upward of 50 percent of the fire from an exploding cap, either because the flame has to travel so far to reach the powder charge, or because only about half of the explosion went down the flash channel of the nipple and bolster arrangement in the first place.

With the in-line percussion rifles, such as the Knight MK-85 and the Thunder Hawk from Thompson/Center Arms, the explosion from a percussion cap has to travel only a fraction of an inch to reach the powder charge. A much hotter flame reaches the powder charge here than with traditional side-hammer muzzleloader designs. In fact, fire from a percussion cap with an in-line ignition system is similar to the fire from the primer of a centerfire cartridge. Ignition is more spontaneous even with CTG grade Pyrodex.

I spent a great deal of time shooting CTG Pyrodex behind a variety of heavy lead conical bullets out of my in-line rifle. Performance was outstanding. Groups were every bit as good as with FFg black powder, sometimes even better. However, when equal charges of FFg black powder and CTG were fired behind a particular bullet, the Pyrodex load tended to print just about an inch lower on the target on average. This indicates that the coarse-grained powder is slightly slower burning than black powder.

As always, I found that wiping fouling from the bore between shots greatly improved accuracy. Additional shooting with Select-grade Pyrodex behind several maxi-type bullets resulted in much better accuracy than I had previously obtained with RS grade. My best groups with Hornady Great Plains bullets and the hollow-pointed Maxi bullets from Buffalo Bullet Company improved significantly when the factory lube was rinsed from the bullets with hot tap water and the bullet was relubed with Hodgdon's own specially formulated Pyrodex lube.

If you know all your shots will be at game within 50 or 60 yards, there's no reason to doubt the effectiveness of the patched round ball. At these distances, a .50- or .54-caliber rifle loaded with a healthy powder charge behind a patched round ball should bring down even the biggest buck cleanly when you put the shot into a vital area. However, **if you feel you may be faced with an occasional shot out to and maybe even a little past 100 yards, seriously consider shooting a rifle that will handle accurately one of the energy retaining conical or saboted handgun bullets.** When hunting open country game like the pronghorn and mule deer, they are a must, and when the target happens to be something as large as an elk or moose, it makes a lot of sense to rely on a bullet that's been designed to give maximum performance.

Whether you load and hunt with black powder or Pyrodex, your first shot will always be your best. So make it count.

Chapter 7

Sighting In & Making The Shot

One question I'm asked more frequently than any other is, "How far can you shoot a deer with a muzzleloader?"

Depending upon the mood I'm in, I reply, "You can't shoot a deer with a muzzleloader very far at all, because they're so tough to stuff down the barrel", or I ask, "You mean shot distance, right?"

When the inquirer shows an honest interest in muzzleloading, I'll normally respond that about 100 yards is the maximum practical distance anyone should consider a shot at any big game animal. On the other hand, if I know I'm talking with someone either just getting into muzzleloading or seriously considering buying his first frontloading rifle, especially for deer hunting, I'll go into more detail and expound upon the virtues of the round ball projectiles at relatively close range and the use of heavier conical bullets at longer ranges. Sometimes I think the lucky guy is the one who gets the "Oh, about a hundred yards" answer.

Although ballistics will vary slightly from one rifle to another of the same caliber, due to variances in tightness of patch and ball fit, brand of black powder used, type of ignition, barrel length and even the rate of rifling twist, this variation isn't so great that each rifle is so much a firearm unto itself. It's easy to quote ballistics, and several good books on muzzleloading have easy-to-read charts showing the velocities and energy of different powder charges in most popular calibers. Anyone who can read can quote ballistics of round ball and conical muzzleloading projectiles and come off sounding like an expert on the subject, possibly with little shooting experience!

An aspect of hunting with a muzzleloading rifle that's a little more difficult to understand without actual field experience is the importance of knowing the exact range of the target. I've had several black powder shooters comment to me that they shoot the same powder charge for 25-, 50- and even 100-yard shooting and don't make any sight allowances for the longer range shooting. Impossible! **Even with an optimum loading, a muzzleloading rifle fires a pronounced rainbow trajectory.**

Where regulations allow, I'll always rely on a scope mounted aboard my favorite muzzleloading whitetail rifle. I'm not a traditionalist, even though a fair share of the 80 whitetails I've taken with a muzzleloader have been with frontloading guns of a

• *The long eye relief handgun scope aboard this custom muzzleloading hunting rifle allowed the author to do a better job of placing his shot on this wide-racked eight-pointer. The buck was taken at 125 yards.*

traditional design.

A good scope makes any rifle much more efficient. Properly sighted, my rig is an effective 150- to 160-yard whitetail rifle. Yeah, I know my standard answer to inquiries is 100 yards, and when you're talking open sights, that is the limit. Besides, when I'm talking to anyone basically unfamiliar with the sport, I'd much rather err on the side of caution. There's absolutely no sense in giving unrealistically optimistic replies.

Since I pack the same rifle I use for whitetails on hunts for other big game, from caribou on the northern tundras to javelina in Texas brush country, I like a scope which offers a high degree of flexibility. A good 3X-9X or 2X-7X model fills the bill.

Scope technology has come a long way over the past couple of decades; you now can buy a well-built scope at a reasonable price. In fact, many of today's mid-price models are much better scopes than the top-of-the-line models 20 years ago. **Like buying a muzzleloading hunting rifle, just try to buy the best model you can afford. Look at optics for your rifle as an investment, not an added expense.**

My rifle presently is fitted with a 3X-9X Nikon with a 40mm front objective lens which does an excellent job of gathering light early in the morning or late in the afternoon. Rarely will I want to use any magnification beyond the two extremes. When I'm hunting in heavy timber or from a tree stand, the scope will be turned down to its lowest setting. When I work along open cornfields or through semi-open pastures, the scope will be cranked all the way up to its highest setting.

A number of experienced modern muzzleloading hunters I know prefer a fixed 4X scope in fear of leaving a variable at too high a setting during a low-power situation. To me, knowing which power the scope is set at is just part of being 100 percent into the hunt. The benefit of higher magnification for those hundred yard-plus shots is worth the effort it takes to remember turning it down when hunting in closer quarters.

Another question I'm often asked as I travel the country giving black powder hunting seminars is how I sight in the modernistic muzzleloader. Just because the rifle looks

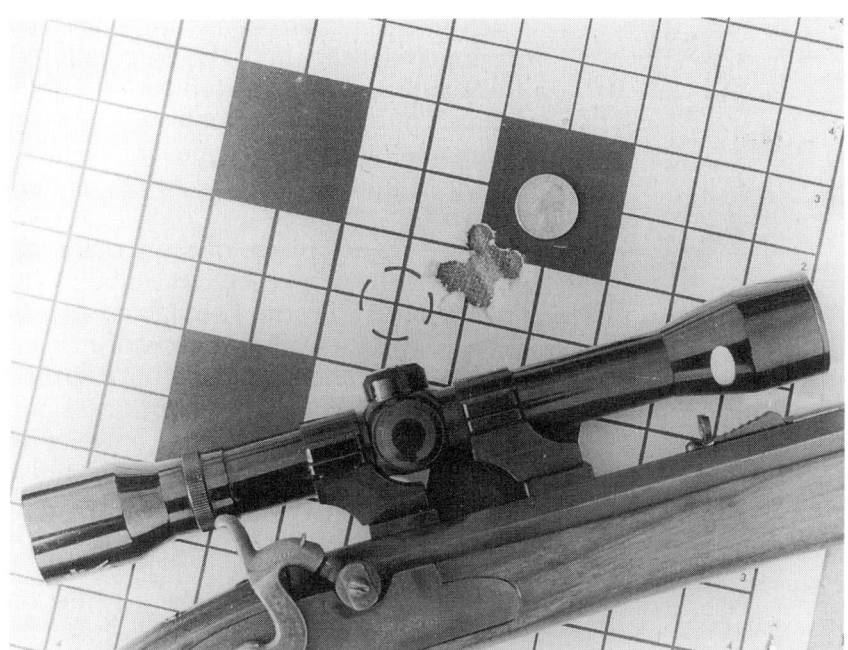

• (Above) A quality scope can help turn almost any muzzleloader into a more effective hunting rifle. This old Tingle half-stock which was built during the 1960s produced this tight 50-yard group with patched round balls.

• The author with a Texas eight-pointer dropped at nearly 130 yards shooting a saboted 260 grain jacketed .45 caliber hollow-point pistol bullet.

Sighting In/Making the Shot

• Bigger is not always better. The author feels that a .50 caliber frontloader is capable of producing all of the energy needed for any North American big game animal, provided it's loaded with the right projectile.

• Heavy conicals such as this deliver tremendous downrange energy but display poor, rainbow trajectories.

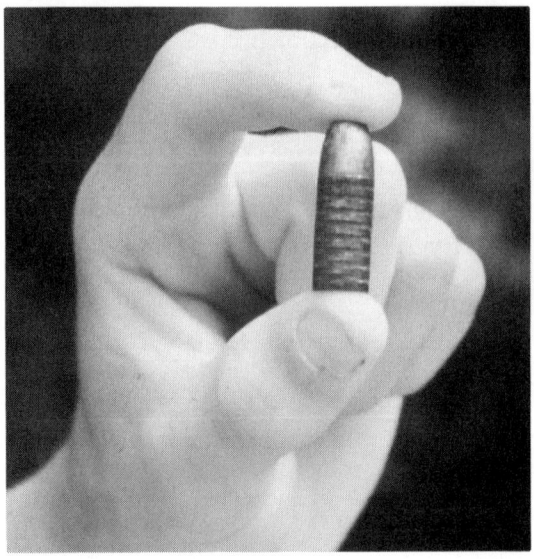

much like a modern centerfire, it still is a black powder firearm. The percussion in-line's maximum effective range still is dictated by the limited ballistics of black powder or Pyrodex, the same limiting factor as with a traditional Hawken or Pennsylvania rifle.

To take advantage of the scope's versatility and the rifle's effectiveness out to and slightly past 150 yards, I've sighted my rifle accordingly. For whitetails, most of the shots I take are well under 75 yards, but each season I find myself faced with an occasional shot at the outermost effective limits of my frontloader. My scope has been sighted to reduce the amount of calculating I have to do, whether the deer is at 50 yards or at 150 yards.

The bigger the caliber of the rifle, the heavier the projectile fired; likewise, the greater the amount of drop at longer range. A .50-caliber Thompson/Center Hawken with a 28-inch barrel length and a hefty 90-grain charge of FFFg behind a patched .495-inch diameter round ball pushes the projectile from the muzzle at just over 1,800 fps. Sighted to hit dead on at 25 yards, at 50 yards the rifle impacts almost 1-1/2 inches low, at 75 yards the drop is nearly four inches and at 100 yards the drop is almost eight inches below point of aim. At 125 yards the .50-caliber rifle prints approximately 14 inches low, at 150 yards the drop is around 22 inches, and, at 200 yards the rifle will print almost 50 inches below the point of aim.

A 100-grain charge of FFFg behind a tightly patched .530 round ball is a good hunting load for most .54-caliber frontloading rifles. In Thompson/Center's .54-caliber version of the Hawken, this load is good for a muzzle velocity of slightly over 1,600 fps out of the rifle's 28-inch barrel. If sighted to hit dead on at 25 yards, just as the .50-caliber rifle was, this rifle will shoot almost two inches low at 50 yards, five inches low at 75 yards and 10 inches below point of aim at 100 yards. Bigger bore rifles may offer more impact (energy), but they also result in considerably more drop at longer ranges.

Heavier conical bullets, such as the

• It is impossible to have any rifle hitting "on" at all ranges. The kill zone of an average whitetail buck normally measures about one foot square. Add excitement and distance judging error and what will you get....the buck or the twig? Photo by Richard P. Smith.

Thompson/Center Maxi-Ball and the Lee Precision R.E.A.L. (Rifling Engraved At Loading) bullets, leave the muzzle of a frontloader at considerably slower velocities than the lighter round ball projectiles when loaded in front of like powder charges. Powder charges of about a third more have to be loaded to push the big 200- to 250-grain .45-caliber slugs, 300-grain and heavier .50-caliber conicals and nearly 500-grain, .54-caliber bullets from the muzzle at velocities approaching that of the round ball. Even with their ballistically superior design, these big slugs result in even more drop than the round ball projectiles due to their heavier weight, often twice that of a proper diameter ball for the same caliber.

A 90-grain charge of FFg pushes a 220-grain Maxi-Ball from the muzzle of a .45-caliber Thompson/Center Hawken rifle at approximately 1,800 fps. Sighted to hit dead on at 25 yards, the rifle will print the big conical approximately seven inches low at 100 yards. A .50-caliber Thompson/Center Hawken firing a 370-grain Maxi-Ball at a similar muzzle velocity (requiring more than 120 grains of FFg) would hit approximately nine inches low at 100 yards if sighted to hit dead on at 25 yards. A 400-grain, .54-caliber Maxi-Ball fired from a 28-inch barreled Hawken rifle at approximately 1,500 fps (requiring 120 grains of FFg) would likewise drop around 10 inches below point of aim if the muzzleloader had been sighted to hit dead on at 25 yards.

No matter whether the rifle is loaded with a patched round ball or a heavy hunting conical, it is impossible to have the rifle hitting "on" at all ranges. The kill zone of the average whitetail buck normally measures around a foot square and covers that part of the rib cage containing the heart, lungs and liver. This sounds like a sizeable target, even at 100 yards, but compound the excitement of the hunt with common human error in sighting and there's not much room left for snap judging of calculated bullet drop. This becomes even more of a problem if the shooter is a poor judge of distance.

There are several reasons I prefer the modern jacketed handgun bullet and sabot over all other muzzleloading projectiles. First, the bullet offers superior expansion and transfer of energy. **Second,** it is extremely accurate when shot from a rifle with the proper rifling. **Third,** when bullet weight

Sighting In/Making the Shot

• *Whether you scope sight your rifle, use a peep sight or open sight, always sight in to take full advantage of the load you hunt with.*

is kept under 300 grains, the trajectory is much flatter than that of the heavy conical muzzleloading bullets.

My personal choice is one of the .45-caliber Speer 260-grain jacketed hollowpoints, loaded into my .50-caliber Knight rifle using one of the black Modern Muzzleloading "Hi-Per Shock" sabots. With 100 grains of Pyrodex "Select", this bullet and sabot combination shoots extremely flat and delivers plenty of punch for taking out the biggest whitetail buck.

Sighted to hit dead on at 100 yards, the load will print just a little shy of 6-1/2 inches low at 150 yards. At 50 yards, the 260-grain slug impacts right at 1-1/2 inches high. So sighted, one of the modern in-line percussion rifles would satisfy most muzzleloading whitetail hunters.

The vast majority of my deer hunting is done in three midwestern states -- Iowa, Illinois and Missouri. Here, I'm just as likely to see a buck at 100 to 150 yards as I am at 35 to 75 yards. My rifle has been sighted to print the jacketed hollow-point three inches high at 100 yards. At 150 yards, the bullet impacts 3-1/2 inches below point of aim, and at 50 yards the shot will be just over four inches high.

So sighted, I can pretty well throw the crosshairs dead center of the chest cavity on any deer that steps out from 50 to 150 yards and effectively drop the buck. A hit three inches high or three inches low still will take out vital organs. The past 35 or so whitetails I've taken with my muzzleloader have been taken with the rifle so sighted, and I've been able to walk to where the vast majority of these deer were standing when shot and see the buck laying less than 20 yards away. Even the two or three which required some trailing traveled less than 50 yards before going down.

Unfortunately, antiquated regulations in many states make it illegal to use a scope aboard a muzzleloader during the muzzleloading seasons. Fortunately, times are changing, and muzzleloading continues to mature into a true hunting sport instead of simply a nostalgic or historic interest. Ten years ago, only a half-dozen or so states allowed the use of a scope during muzzleloading seasons. Today, the number of states allowing telescopic sights is around 20, and I know of at least two or three others now considering a regulation change to allow scopes aboard muzzleloaders.

Whether you scope your muzzleloading deer rifle or not, always sight in to take full advantage of the load you hunt with. The limited effective range of a patched round ball will allow the hunter to sight more dead on than with any other projectile. Sighted dead on at 50 yards with a hefty hunting charge, a .50- or .54- caliber rifle will print a round ball only about an inch high at 25 yards and less than two inches low at 75. Beyond that, the knowledgeable black powder hunter should realize that a round ball just doesn't deliver enough punch to do the job.

While heavy conicals will maintain energy levels high enough to take whitetails out to and past 150 yards, their terrible rainbow trajectory makes it difficult to capitalize on the killing power. Sighted to hit dead on at 100 yards, the great hunks of lead weighing upward of 400 grains drop considerably at 150 yards.

There are a number of variables which can and will affect how a muzzleloading rifle performs from day to day, sometimes from shot to shot. Learning to cope with these variables is the key to being satisfied with the performance you get from any muzzleloading hunting rifle.

● *The efficiency — or inefficiency — of the ignition system can mean the difference between acceptable groups and erratic shots.*

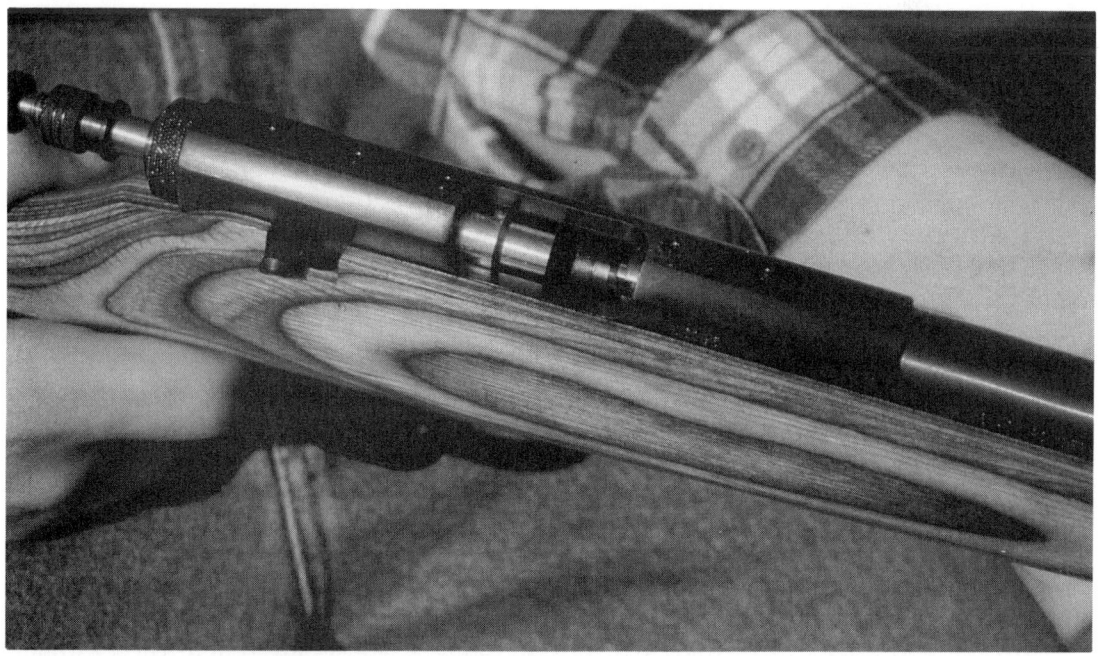

Sighting In/Making the Shot

The efficiency of the ignition system itself can mean the difference between tight, acceptable groups and erratic shot placement. Several years ago I did a great deal of shooting across the sky screens of an Oehler chronograph to compare my findings with the published ballistics of several muzzleloading gun companies. Shooting the same loads as they, I often achieved as much as 100 fps additional velocities.

What I also discovered was that when shooting a percussion rifle I could gain upward of 20 fps simply by replacing the standard nipple with a vented nipple, such as the Uncle Mike's "Hot Shot" design. The nipple helps eliminate compression of the fire from an exploding percussion cap, resulting in more fire into the powder charge. The more positive ignition of the vented nipple also resulted in less deviation in velocity from shot to shot. The sure-fire ignition of percussion in-line rifles offers even better ignition with a system that shortens the travel of the fire from a cap to less than 1/4 inch. Ignition is spontaneous and velocities more consistent, which usually translates to better accuracy downrange.

Sure-fire ignition, high-quality trigger and good sights are all for naught unless the rifle has a barrel with inherent accuracy potential.

The barrels found on today's muzzleloading rifles are rifled using one of four methods. The easiest process is known as "button" rifling. This method literally compresses the grooves of the rifling into the metal by hydraulically pulling an extremely hard "button" through the length of a barrel blank in which the bore has been deep-drilled and polished. The button turns as it is pulled through the smooth bore, creating the rate of rifling twist.

Since the grooves are swaged into the metal, button-rifled barrels feature relatively shallow .004-inch to .005-inch rifling grooves. A broach rifled barrel relies on a stepped button or a series of buttons which can increase the depth of the grooves slightly and can produce a slightly better quality barrel since the grooves aren't compressed to their full depth with a single pass of a single button. Either way, button or broach rifled barrels must utilize a fairly soft steel for the grooves to be uniformly formed as the button or broach is pulled through the bore.

The third rifling process is to hammer forge the barrel around a mandrel. Here a hardened mandrel with raised rotating ribs running its full length is inserted into the slightly oversized bore of a barrel blank. Huge sophisticated forges then hammer the barrel to form both the outside shape plus compress the barrel around the mandrel. When the mandrel is pulled from the barrel, the long ribs leave rifling behind. When care is taken and quality equipment and steels are used, this process can produce a high quality barrel with any practical muzzleloading groove depth desired.

The best muzzleloading barrels are produced using what is referred to as the "cut-rifling" process. A barrel blank is first deep-drilled, then the rough bore is polished, and the rifling formed by pulling a precision cutter through the bore. Each pass of the cutter removes as little as a hundred thousandths of an inch of metal, and a top-quality barrel can require as many as 150 to 160 passes of the cutter to form eight-groove rifling of .005-inch to .006-inch depth. Since the metal is precisely shaved away by a hardened cutter, high tensile strength ordnance grade steels can be used.

A muzzleloading rifle is only as good as the quality of its barrel. Sure-fire ignition, excellent feel and high-quality trigger and sights are all for naught unless a rifle is built with a barrel that has inherent accuracy potential. If you want to hit what you're shooting at, buy the best muzzleloader you can afford. A quality barrel costs more to produce and will add to the cost of the rifle. It's that simple.

My favorite muzzleloading whitetail rifle, a percussion in-line job, will produce slightly better groups at 100 yards when shooting a 100-grain charge of FFg black powder behind one of the saboted .45-caliber jacketed handgun bullets. However, I still rely on Pyrodex for all my hunting loads since the substitute powder lets me reload two, three or four times without "having" to take time to wipe the bore of fouling. (Refer to the chapter on "Working Up Hunting Loads" for a comparison of Pyrodex with black powder.)

Since the mid-1980s, we've seen a real shift in preference toward shorter barrel lengths. For years, muzzleloading experts preached that it took a barrel of at least 28 or 30 inches to obtain the performance needed to produce the ballistics required for hunting deer and other big game. Today, we know better.

It's true that a longer barrel will produce higher velocities and energy levels, but not enough to warrant a hunter handicapping himself with a cumbersome, long-barreled frontloader. One thing that is not hampered in the least by barrels of 20 to 24 inches is accuracy. That is, provided the rifle is equipped with a quality rifled barrel to begin with.

The 260-grain, .45-caliber jacketed hollow-point bullet and sabot combination I shoot in my personal hunting rifle develops a muzzle velocity of about 1,650 fps out of the rifle's 24-inch barrel. The same load in a 28-inch barreled Thompson/Center Hawken rifle results in velocities closer to 1,750 fps. However, the fast one-turn-in-28 inches rate of twist of the cut rifling in the Knight barrel is more compatible with the saboted bullet than the one-turn-in-48 inches rifling of the Thompson/Center Hawken's button rifled barrel, producing better downrange accuracy. Even though the same load out of the longer-barreled Hawken generates about 50 foot-pounds of additional energy, I prefer the rifle which lets me best place the bullet exactly where it needs to go.

Many black powder hunters still are faced with using open sights during the special muzzleloading seasons. However, more and more states are now allowing a scope to be used, and where regulations permit the use of optical sights, hunters are making the switch. Where regulations still

• *Know how your rifle prints up close and at long distances, because you never know where the next shot opportunity will come from. Photo by Gary Clancy.*

Sighting In/Making the Shot

require the use of open sights, or if a hunter prefers open sights, a muzzleloader still can be sighted to take full advantage of all the range a load will give. The key is not to try to take shots beyond your ability to shoot accurately with open sights.

Most of today's reproduction muzzleloaders and all of those models which have been designed specifically for today's black powder hunter feature a quality adjustable rear sight. When adjusting a rear sight, just keep in mind to move it in the direction you want the shot to go. If you want your rifle to shoot higher, move the rear sight up; if you want the shot to go left, move the sight to the left, and so forth.

A high-quality receiver or "peep" sight can be a good option where shots can approach a hundred yards, but where regulations still won't allow the use of a scope. As a rule, such sights are considerably more precise than standard open rear sights. However, their downside is that the small aperture opening can make for difficult sighting during low light conditions. Some hunters screw out the small aperture unit and sight with just the outside housing.

No matter how you sight in your muzzleloading deer rifle, shoot it at all different distances to know how it prints up close and out to where you feel is the maximum effective range of the load you're using. Even the hottest and most modern loads for today's frontloading hunting rifles still have a pronounced trajectory when compared to that of a centerfire rifle. Knowing how your rifle shoots at all ranges is the key to success in the deer woods.

Chapter 8

Ten Steps To Better Muzzleloading Rifle Accuracy

"Powder before patch and ball...or it won't shoot at all!"

Muzzleloading shooters from eras past once adopted sayings such as this to remind themselves to pour in a powder charge before starting a patched ball or bullet and ramming it down the bore. When loaded into a dry, clean bore, and with good ignition, any powder and projectile combination stuffed down the bore in the right sequence should fire. However, getting a muzzleloading rifle to shoot accurately can be a different story.

The customer service departments of most muzzleloading rifle manufacturers receive calls daily from rifle owners who just can't get their rifles to perform up to their expectations. All too often, many of these rifles end up back at the factory or with the importer, and when checked out by someone knowledgeable in loading and shooting a muzzleloader, a high number will turn in acceptable performance. Just as often as not, the customer's inexperience turns out to be the main reason for poor accuracy.

Anyone purchasing a frontloader of reasonable quality should expect more than just fire and smoke from the rifle. If you are contemplating buying a muzzleloader, or have just purchased a black powder rifle, or even if you have owned one for some time and are less than happy with how accurately it shoots, the following "Ten Steps To Better Muzzleloading Rifle Accuracy" should benefit you.

1) Buy the best rifle you can afford.

Never is the old adage, "You get what you pay for" more applicable than when buying a muzzleloading rifle. Remember, not all frontloading rifles are created equal.

The higher price tag of some models covers added features such as a better grade of wood in the stock, maybe a more elaborate finish on metal parts, or perhaps the added flash of fancy brass or German silver furniture. Quality is another feature which will also cost extra. If your primary concern with the rifle you are buying or have already purchased is accuracy, quality is the feature you need to concentrate on the most.

Such features as a higher quality barrel, a more dependable lock mechanism, and a good trigger with a crisp letoff will push the cost of a rifle up there. For any manufacturer to turn out a bargain priced rifle, some features have to be compromised. In short, don't expect a $150 rifle to perform as well as a $300 rifle.

2) Consider the projectile to be shot.

• Buy the best rifle you can afford. It is a hunting investment, not an expense.
Photo by Gary Clancy.

• Consider the projectile to be shot. You can't expect the same results from a patched round ball and a conical or sabot.

Ten Steps to Accuracy

• *This Navy Arms piece is an extremely high quality rifle designed to shoot the patched round ball. All the experimenting in the world won't make it shoot a "maxi" style conical bullet.*

While a number of rifles currently on the market have been promoted as being ideal for either the patched round ball or conical projectiles, there is no such thing as an all-purpose bore which will shoot both admirably. Before buying a muzzleloading rifle, decide right at the outset which type of projectile you intend to shoot. It takes an entirely different bore to obtain the absolute best accuracy from either the round ball or heavy conical.

Keep in mind that accuracy with a patched ball is based upon a paradox -- an undersized sphere of lead spun by rifling it never actually touches. It is the important role of the patch to grasp the pure lead ball, while at the same time ride the grooves of the rifling to transfer the spin of the grooves to the ball.

Ideal rifling for shooting a patched round ball would feature a slow one-turn-in-60 to -72 inches, with grooves of at least .007-inch deep. A twist this slow offers little resistance to a patched ball, especially in a bore with deep enough grooves to accommodate a compressed heavy patch. When a ball is loaded into a fast twist bore with shallow grooves, it may have a tendency to "skip" or "strip" the rifling. In other words, the ball may travel down the bore so fast it resists being spun by the rifling.

Conical bullets like the Thompson/Center Maxi-Ball and Maxi-Hunter, Connecticut Valley Arms "Deerslayer" bullet, or Hornady Great Plains bullet can be up to twice as long as they are in diameter, requiring a much faster rate of twist to stabilize the bullets in flight. Rifles such as the Knight MK-85 or CVA "Apollo" have been specifically designed to shoot conical bullets and feature rifling which spins with exceptionally fast one-turn-in-28 and -32 inches respectively. The grooves found in these bores are also closer to .005-inch depth, allowing the soft lead conical bullets to expand easily into the bottoms of the grooves for a precise fit with the bore at the instant of ignition. These rifles shoot well with bore diameter conical bullets, but generally perform even better with the saboted handgun bullets.

Buying a rifle that has been designed to shoot the type of bullet you intend to hunt, target shoot or just plink with is as important as the overall quality of the rifle. Don't expect a round ball barrel to group heavy lead conical or saboted bullets well, nor a fast twist conical bullet barrel to turn in its best performance with a patched round ball.

3) Check rifling for rough or overly sharp edges.

Many old timers felt that a muzzleloading rifle had to be shot several hundred times before it would begin to turn in it's best accuracy. This "seasoning" of the bore had nothing to do with tempering the steel of the barrel with a miracle burnt-in finish. This break-in period wore away rough, wiry or overly sharp edges on the lands of the rifling.

Accuracy with the patched round ball is more easily affected by the roughness or sharpness of a new bore. These areas tend to cut or rip slits in the patch, which may let gases from the powder charge burn through the patch and affect accuracy. There's no way a damaged patch can fulfill its important role of sealing off the pressures of the burning powder charge and adequately transfer the spin of the rifling to the ball. While conicals aren't affected nearly as much, accuracy will also be off a little with these big bullets when such conditions exist in the bore.

If you're having trouble with accuracy when shooting a patched round ball, try re-covering a few spent patches to determine if your rifling is damaging the patch. Fired patches usually can be found less than 10 yards from the muzzle. Look for tattletale

> *Rough or sharp edges easily can be taken care of through a simple bore lapping procedure.*

slits which will indicate a problem with the edges of lands. If you shoot a conical bullet but suspect there's something not right about the rifling, check by slowly pushing a tight fitting cleaning patch down the bore. A rough edge will pull at the patch, and you should be able to feel it through the ramrod. Lands with sharp edges shouldn't affect conical accuracy.

Rough or sharp edges easily can be taken care of through a simple bore lapping procedure, which is nothing more than polishing the bore to get rid of sharp or rough edges on the rifling. If the condition is slight, try running a dampened cleaning patch sprinkled with a common bathroom scouring powder through the bore 50 to 100 times. If the condition persists, lap the bore with a tight patch that has been dabbed with valve-grinding compound (available from just about any auto parts store). When lapping the bore with either, always be sure to complete the stroke and push the patch all the way to the bottom of the bore, then pull it all the way back to the muzzle. Before shooting the rifle, give it a thorough cleaning to remove all the abrasive powder or compound.

4) Load and shoot the proper diameter projectiles.

One of the most common mistakes made by the beginning black powder shooter is to try loading with a projectile that's not suitable for his or her rifle. When you're first starting with a new rifle, stick with the ball or bullet diameters recommended by the rifle manufacturer.

When loading with a patched round ball, keep in mind that, for best accuracy, not just any ol' patch and ball combination which will fit through the muzzle will turn in good performance. To fit into the bore, the ball has to be smaller in diameter than land to land measurement of the rifling. Most rifle makers recommend a ball that's .010-inch undersized (.490 inch in a .50 caliber, .530 inch in a .54, etc.), which will leave room for patching of around .010- to .020-inch thickness (depending on the bore).

On the other hand, a conical bullet is loaded into the bore without patching of any sort (except for the modern handgun bullets loaded into some barrels using a plastic sabot). If a bullet drops right in without any resistance whatsoever, it's too small in diameter. If it fits this loosely, it just as easily can slide forward off the powder charge when the rifle is held muzzle down. Any bullet that is not properly seated firmly over the powder charge can cause the powder charge to create erratic pressures as it burns, destroying accuracy. If a bullet slides too far forward it can create hazardous barrel pressures much like any barrel obstruction can cause the barrel to burst.

A good conical bullet design will allow the base and maybe even a middle "bearing band" to be inserted into the bore at the muzzle with little, if any, resistance. A slightly oversize band around the nose of the bullet will then have to be lightly engraved with the rifling when the bullet is pushed into the bore with the aid of a short starter.

If the ball or bullet you're loading is badly deformed by the time you force it into the muzzle of the rifle, it's simply of too large diameter for your rifle. Occasionally, a rifle leaves a manufacturer's facility with a "tight bore", a bore that's slightly undersized. However, in most cases when a ball or bullet loads too tightly, it simply means that the bullet is oversized (in diameter). A switch to a different bullet that has been designed for shooting in your rifle normally will take care of the problem. When you're shooting a patched round ball, be sure the patch being used isn't too thick. Commercially available patches are offered in .005-, .010-, .015- and .020-inch thicknesses. A switch to a thinner material will insure easier loading and often better accuracy.

5) Remove all oil and solvent from bore before loading.

The number one cause of misfires or hang-fires is oil or solvent left in the bore from a previous cleaning. When a small reservoir of fluid rests between the ignition system and the powder charge, it's unlikely that enough fire will reach the powder charge to insure positive, sure-fire ignition.

Before loading a flintlock rifle, be sure to run several dry patches down the bore to remove all traces of oil or solvent. With a percussion rifle, do the same. Then snap several caps on the rifle, push another clean, dry patch down the bore and leave it there. Snap several more caps. Pull out the ramrod and check the cleaning patch. If the bore is receiving good fire through the ignition system the patch will reveal a large burnt area. It also indicates that all oil has been wiped and burnt out of the breech end of the barrel.

6) Load with consistent powder charges.

Fortunately, black powder can be forgiving. When loading with a volume type measure, it's not uncommon for the actual weight of powder charges to vary five to ten percent. In a larger .50- or .54-caliber rifle, this usually isn't enough to present a problem. However, in the smaller bore rifles it can create enough change in impact to

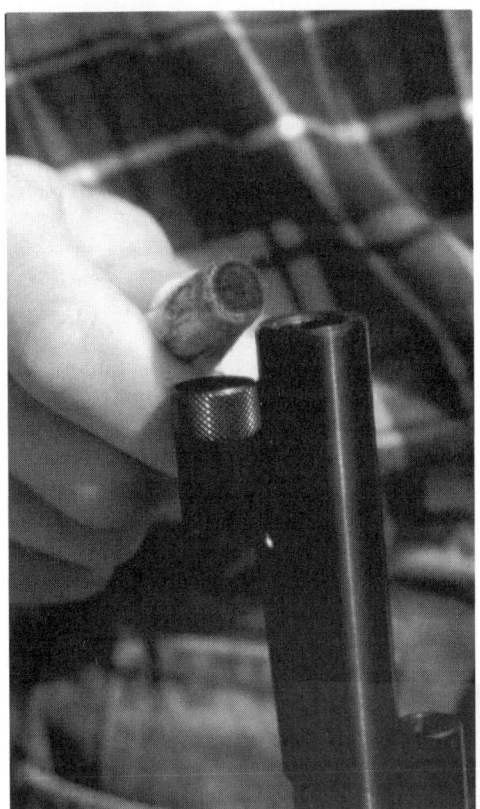

• *One way to determine whether you're getting good fire through to the barrel is to push the cleaning jag with a patch down onto the face of the breechplug and snap several caps. If fire is reaching the barrel, the patch will show a burn spot.*

• *Before loading any percussion muzzleloader, always take time to snap a cap or two on the nipple to blow and burn oil or cleaning solvents from the ignition system.*

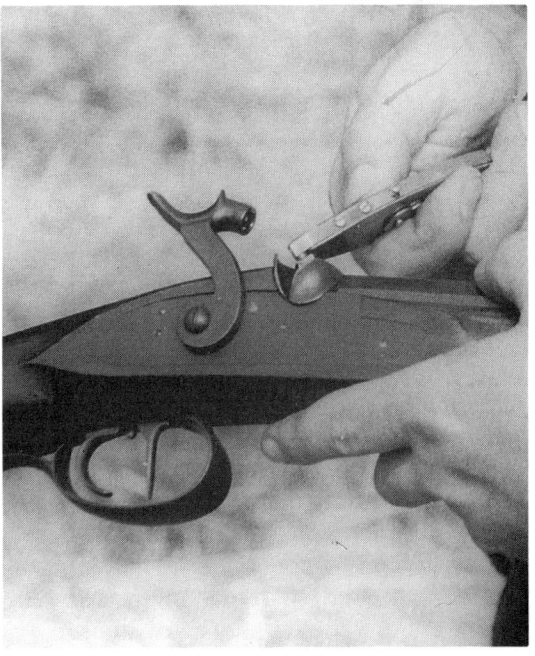

Ten Steps to Accuracy

• Beating a projectile into the bore as this shooter is doing only deforms the ball or bullet and destroys accuracy.

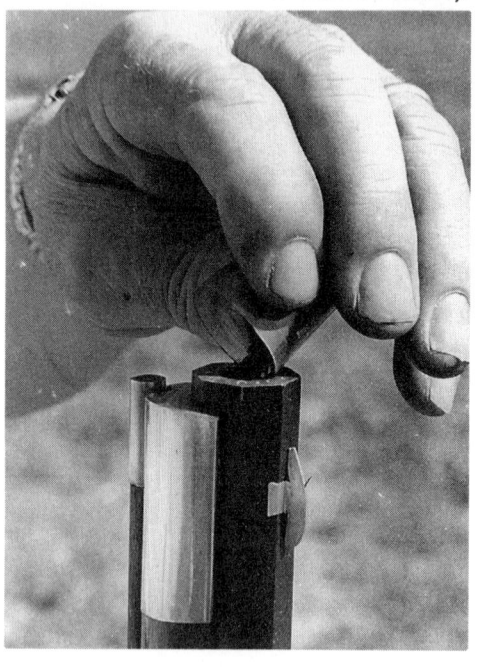

• When loading and shooting a muzzleloader, learn to do things the same each time. Consistency has its reward — consistent accuracy.

cause a shooter to miss a squirrel's head at just 25 yards.

Powder charges can be made much more consistent by tapping the side of the powder measure lightly as it is being filled from the flask or powder horn. This causes the powder to settle in the measure nearly the same from load to load. The result will be powder charges that are closer to the same each time, which equates to a tighter downrange group.

7) Seat the projectile with the same amount of pressure each time.

Although consistent powder charges of a consistent grain size are extremely important to maintaining shot placement with little variation from shot to shot, how the projectile is seated over the powder charge also can be an influencing factor. It's extremely important that the same amount of pressure be placed on the ramrod when loading for each shot. This is especially true when loading a patched round ball, but can still affect the extreme spread of impact points when shooting any of the big conical-type bullets.

A number of serious target shooters have experimented with this, often going to the extreme of taking a bathroom scale to the range with them. When loading the projectile, the rifle butt would be placed on the scale and the same number of pounds of pressure exerted on the projectile each time. The more consistent the pressure, the better the accuracy. Believe it or not, it can take

• *A quality trigger, or set of triggers, is nearly as important to accuracy as good ignition.*

upward of 80 pounds of pressure to consistently seat a ball over the powder charge.

Most shooters can develop a "feel" for the amount of pressure being exerted on the ramrod and can be surprisingly consistent even without the aid of a bathroom scale (which still is a good way to determine just how much pressure you should be using). The important thing is to use the same amount of pressure each time.

One of the old wive's tales of muzzleloading was that a shooter should "bounce" his ramrod on the bullet once it was seated over the powder charge. The thought was that if the ramrod bounced back, then the bullet or ball was properly seated. If the ramrod didn't bounce back, then the projectile still was not seated directly atop the powder. Well, don't do it! All bouncing the ramrod accomplishes is to deform the nose of the bullet, which will make it tougher to get consistent accuracy from your rifle.

8) Wipe fouling from the bore between shots.

Fouling build-up in the bore can greatly influence muzzleloading ballistics and accuracy. When the bore of a black powder rifle is not wiped between shots, velocities will continue to rise with each succeeding shot. The fouling build-up creates greater pressures. This inconsistency from shot to shot has an adverse affect on accuracy.

To maintain accuracy, run either a solvent or saliva-dampened patch down the bore after each shot. The idea is not to thoroughly clean the bore, but to keep fouling from building up. You'll also find it a lot easier to seat a projectile each time when you wipe the bore between shots.

9) Shoot a good trigger.

Even if your rifle is equipped with the most dependable lock and a barrel featuring quality rifling, it's doubtful that you'll be able to obtain consistent accuracy if your trigger isn't of the same quality. A trigger with a clean, crisp break is an absolute must.

The quality of the trigger (or triggers) found on today's mass produced reproduction rifles runs from poor to very acceptable. This all goes back to the first step to muzzleloading accuracy...buying the best quality you can afford. Target quality trig-

Ten Steps to Accuracy

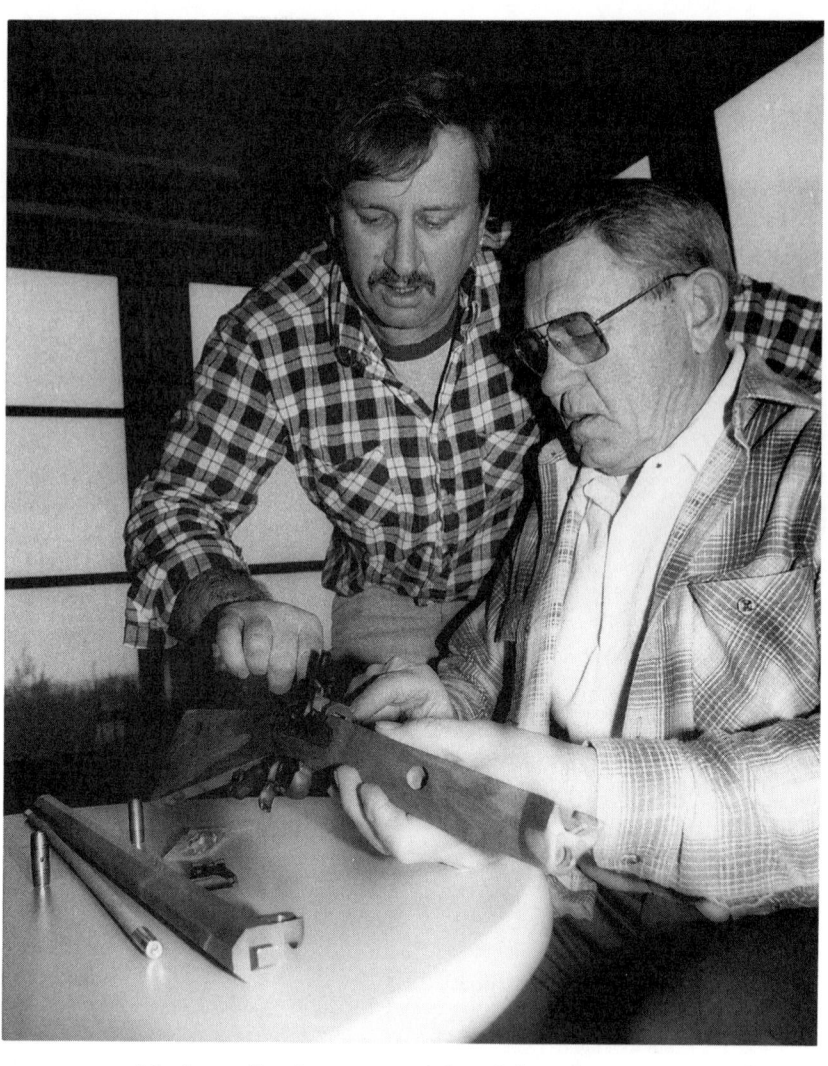

• *Purchasing a kit and putting the rifle together yourself can help save money. Photo by Gary Clancy.*

gers aren't cheap and to tamper with the pull weight of triggers that come with many reproduction rifles will void the warranty.

Even if you're on an extremely tight budget, try to wait until you can afford a rifle that comes equipped with an adjustable set of "double-set" triggers, or at least comes with some sort of adjustment to get trigger pull down to around three pounds. Those triggers which have no trigger travel are another step up. If the trigger or triggers on the rifle you may already own are hopeless, there are quality commercial triggers available which possibly could be fitted to your rifle. This may require the services of a good gunsmith.

10) Shoot often and don't be afraid to experiment with loads.

Improved accuracy with a muzzleloading rifle often is the result of doing considerable shooting with the frontloader. The more powder you put through the bore of your rifle, the more accustomed you become to the rifle's lock, trigger, sights, etc. The more you shoot, the more refined your load often becomes.

It's this fine tuning of a rifle's performance which makes you a better shot. **Every muzzleloader is something of an individual.** Two rifles that are identical in every way may each prefer slightly different loads. For this reason, never accept another shooter's load as the best load for your rifle. Finding the optimum load for your rifle may require hundreds of rounds, trying different types of bullets, ball diameters, patch thicknesses, or even type of powder (black powder or Pyrodex). Just remember never to exceed a manufacturer's recommended maximum powder charge.

Shoot often in practice... so you'll need to shoot only once at the quarry!

Checklist For Quality

Use the following checklist to determine whether the muzzleloading rifle you are looking to buy meets the criteria for a "serious" muzzleloading hunting rifle:

- ❑ Does the rifle have a quality barrel with good rifling?
- ❑ Is the barrel rifled with a rifling twist which will perform well with the type of projectile you intend to shoot?
- ❑ Are projectiles readily available, or does manufacturer require the use of only "their" bullets?
- ❑ Does the lock mechanism operate smoothly?
- ❑ Will the ignition system give positive, sure-fire ignition?
- ❑ If the rifle is a modern in-line percussion model, are the safeties positive and easy to engage/disengage quietly?
- ❑ Does the rifle feature a good adjustable rear sight?
- ❑ Are scope-mount bases and rings readily available, making scope

mounting easy?
- ❏ Is the trigger fully adjustable?
- ❏ Is the rifle of an adequate caliber for the game to be hunted?
- ❏ Does the rifle have acceptable weight and balance?
- ❏ Are the stock and butt of a design which will be comfortable when you're shooting hefty hunting charges and projectiles?
- ❏ Can the rifle be cleaned easily?
- ❏ What is the presence and quality of other features, such as sling swivel studs, sturdiness of ramrod, etc.?
- ❏ What is the manufacturer's warranty and service policy?

• *Into each life some rain must fall.... and into many hunts, snow will fall. You and your gear must be ready. Photo by Tom Fegely.*

Chapter 9

Muzzleloaders Must Be Cleaned!

To say blackpowder shooting is messy is putting it lightly. The fouling left after each shot continues to build until it becomes impossible to load any manner of muzzleloading gun. This fouling not only cakes the bore, it can be found on metal areas around the ignition system, ahead of the cylinder of a percussion revolver, and even on the sides of the barrel at the muzzle. You'll be surprised at the amount of this residue you'll also find on yourself!

Cleaning blackpowder fouling from your hands, or the dab that may get on your face and clothing, requires only a good washing. Similarly, cleaning it from your favorite frontloader requires only a good scrubbing.

Blackpowder is easily broken down with water. Many frontiersmen had nothing but water to clean the barrels of their muzzleloaders. Safe from the impending dangers of his often-hostile environment, the backwoodsman would quickly strip down his rifle, swab the bore with a number of water-soaked patches, and if a good fire were at hand and water could be boiled, pour the bore full of boiling water. This wasn't so much an attempt to get that last little bit of fouling out as it was a way to heat the metal of the barrel, so that after a couple of dry patches were used to wipe the bore fairly dry, the heated metal could air dry quickly and thoroughly. He then would use an oiled patch to put a light rust-preventing coat of lube on the cleaned metal surface.

While blackpowder breaks down with water, the residue left behind by patch lubes, especially by some of today's modern concoctions, may not. Hot soapy water has become a favorite solution with many of today's blackpowder shooters. The hot water easily breaks down the powder residue and heats the metal for fast drying, while the detergent works on the residue left behind by patch or bullet lube. The hot, soapy solution does an excellent job of keeping a muzzleloader bore spotless, but it's not always handy. Fortunately, a number of manufacturers presently market a variety of solvents that are a lot handier to pack in the field or use in the hunting camp.

One of the most effective commercial blackpowder solvents available, and one that's been around quite a few years, is Birchwood Casey's No. 77. This is a water-based solvent that does a great job of keeping a hunting rifle clean away from the luxu-

- One shot with a muzzleloader is all it takes to require that the rifle be thoroughly cleaned at the end of the day. Both black powder and Pyrodex are corrosive. (Above photo)

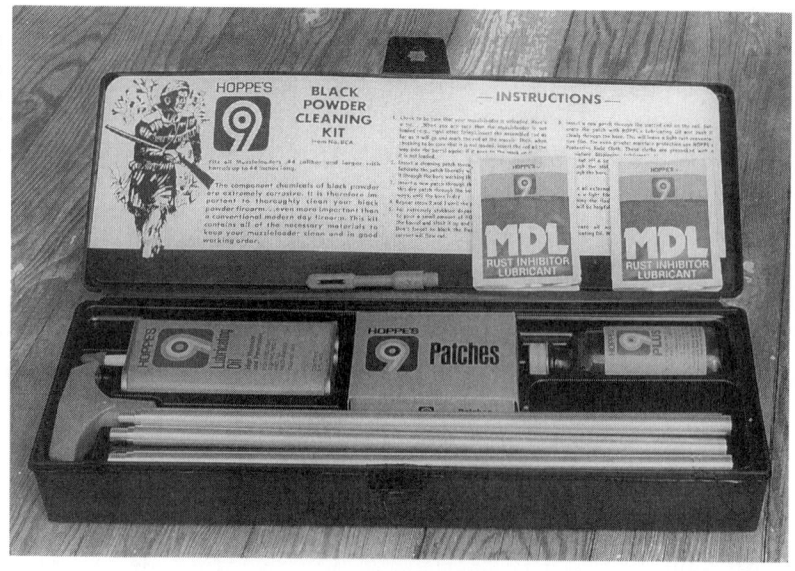

- A number of suppliers offer handy black powder cleaning kits which make it easy to purchase everything needed to keep a frontloader in top working condition.

- Many of the Hawken designs allow the barrel to be removed for cleaning by tapping out a wedge through the forestock and a tenon on the bottom of the barrel.

Must Be Cleaned

• Hot, soapy water poured down the barrel is step number one in cleaning the fouling. Photo by Richard P. Smith.

ries of home. However, I've found it a good idea to really give a favorite frontloader a thorough going over after being out and about with it for a week and use the No. 77 solvent to clean the bore while away.

Birchwood Casey's solvent is especially good for keeping fouling out of the bore when working up loads or sighting in. Just run a No. 77-dampened patch down the bore and back out between shots. Succeeding shots load as easily as the first round in a clean bore. Following a shooting session, run a half-dozen No. 77-soaked patches down the bore, then run four or five dry patches down the bore to dry the metal of any of the water-based lube remaining.

Another patch saturated with lube coats the metal and prevents rust from forming until you return home that evening and give the rifle a thorough scrubbing. A patch dampened with No. 77 also can be used to wipe away residue on the outside of the gun, followed by a coat of lube.

Shooter's Choice Black Powder Gel, Rusty Duck Black-Off and Hoppe's No. 9 Plus are just a few of the other brand names of commercially produced cleaning solvents. All can, and will, thoroughly clean the bore of a hunting muzzleloader. When in hunting camp for only a few days, or even a week, don't really scrub the bore of the gun until you return home. The more often and thoroughly the gun is cleaned, the greater chance you take of getting some of the lube into the flash channel of a percussion system, and to a smaller degree, the vent of a flintlock. A better idea is lightly to dampen a patch or two and wipe the excess fouling from the bore at the end of the day — just enough to make loading for the

• *A cleaning jag is a must for any frontloading rifle.*

next day's hunt easier. However, if the weather is bad, a thorough cleaning may be necessary to keep the gun from rusting.

The fact remains, however, that following a hunt, the muzzleloader used must have a thorough cleaning. It's one of the necessary evils of enjoying blackpowder guns!

As a charge of black powder burns down the length of a bore, it leaves behind a heavy residue or fouling on the inside barrel wall. With each succeeding shot, this fouling builds. Unless the bore is wiped occasionally — after every three or four shots — this residue can build to the point where loading the gun is impossible, especially when shooting a tight ball and patch combination. The smaller the bore, the faster it fouls. Some of the .32- and .36- caliber rifles should be wiped with a saliva-dampened patch between every shot.

Fouling also increases the chance of snapping a wooden ramrod as you try to muscle a patched ball or conical bullet down an extremely fouled bore. It also increases the chance of sticking a projectile partially down the barrel. The smart shooter tries to go ahead and seat the bullet over the powder, with whatever it takes, or takes the gun to a competent gunsmith and has the bullet removed.

This can be done by pulling a ball with a specially tipped ramrod that screws into the soft lead bullet, or it may require unbreeching the gun and tapping the bullet back out the direction from which it was stuffed. The shooter not so indoctrinated in shooting blackpowder guns foolishly may attempt to go ahead and shoot out the stuck projectile. With considerable air space between powder charge and bullet, the projectile could cause the barrel to burst, the same as with any other barrel obstruction.

As fouling builds in a muzzleloading rifle's bore, identical powder charges produce higher and higher pressures, because it simply takes more power to get the projectile moving down the dirty bore. Although such increases in pressure are hardly dangerous, as long as reasonable powder charges are being shot and the projectile is seated all the way down on top of the powder charge, these variations destroy accu-

• *Some of the newer in-line rifles have a removable breech plug. You don't need to shoot the rifle to unload it at the end of the day. Just remove the plug and punch out the bullet.*

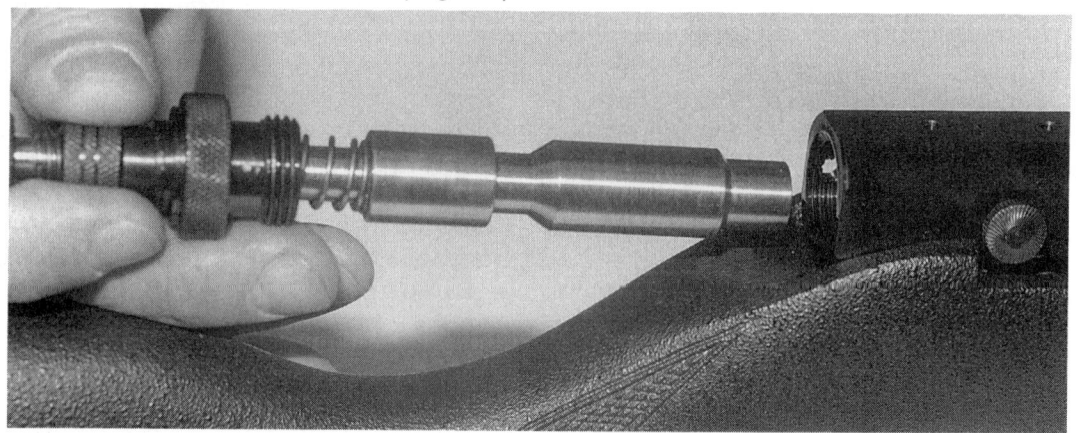

• *Cleaning a muzzleloader in a spike camp on an elk hunt. Photo by Gary Clancy.*

racy. **Cleanliness just might be next to godliness, and in a muzzleloader it's also conducive to accuracy and safety.**

Some of today's reproduction muzzleloading rifles feature a patent, or hooked, breeching system. These easily can be broken down for cleaning by tapping one or two wedges from the wedgeplates located on the forestock and a corresponding tenon on the bottom of the barrel, then lifting the barrel from the muzzle end until the hook of the breech plug disengages a recess in the face of the tang. The barrel can be removed in a few seconds if the wedges aren't too stubborn. Several firms presently produce a handy little wedge tool that can make tearing down a rifle with stubborn wedges a snap.

With the barrel removed, the breech end then can be stuck down into a bucket of cleaning solution. Inserting a damp patch into the muzzle with a tight-fitting jag threaded to the end of the cleaning rod forces the compressed air in the barrel back out the nipple of a percussion rifle or the vent of a flint rifle as the rod and jag are pushed downward. When the rod and jag are pulled back toward the muzzle, the solution is drawn back into the barrel. When the rod goes back down, the solution is forced back out. A dozen or so good strokes will generally clean just about any bore spotless.

Traditionally, the barrels of some Kentucky rifles, and those of several other styles,

Must Be Cleaned

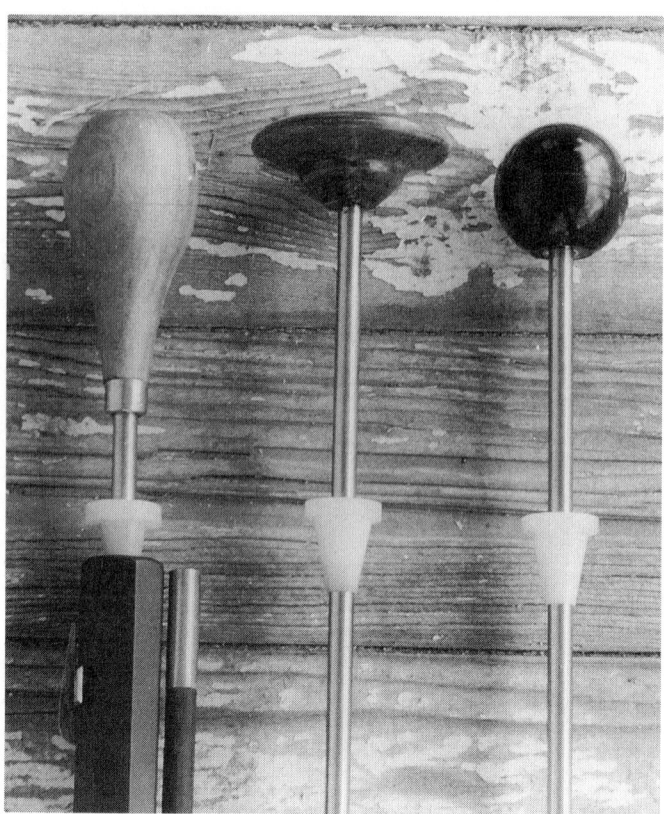

- *Auxiliary cleaning rods come in various styles and lengths. They will save wear and tear on your ramrod.*

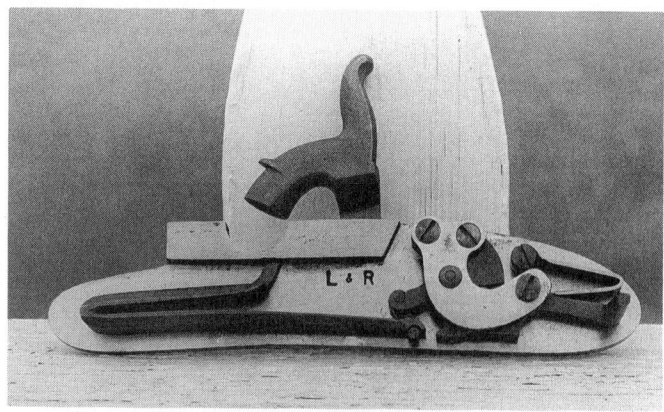

- *Cleaning a muzzleloading rifle also means keeping the inside of the lock mechanism clean. Black powder fouling can find its way to internal parts and ruin a quality lock.*

- *Poor maintenance and improper cleaning lead to the destruction of this reproduction flintlock rifle.*

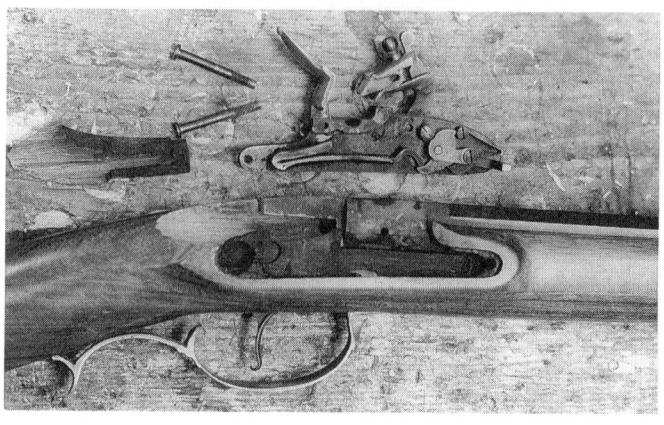

Must Be Cleaned

• *A comfortable hunting camp offers most of the comforts of home and the conveniences for keeping a muzzleloader clean during the course of a hunt.*

are pinned in place along the forestock. Removing these barrels for cleaning is often impossible. Since the pins were made for a tight fit through the tenons on the bottom of the barrel, it is not recommended that the barrels on these guns be removed for cleaning. Removed and replaced several times, the pins would likely become loose fitting and could be lost. Those frontloaders with permanently attached (pinned) barrels either can be cleaned from the muzzle or through the vent or flash channel of the ignition system itself.

Percussion rifles can be cleaned easily by slipping a short piece of tight-fitting surgical hose or aquarium air pump tubing over the cone of the nipple, then dropping the other end of the tube into a bucket of cleaning solution. The solution will be drawn through the tubing and into the bore by the suction created when a tight-fitting patch and jag are pulled back toward the muzzle. A downward stroke will push the solvent back out through the tube and into the bucket. Several companies offer elaborate setups of this type that provide a more watertight cleaning system. Whether the commercial flush tube systems are used or a piece of small diameter tubing simply slipped into place, the arrangement allows a pinned-in barrel to be cleaned in nearly the same manner as those guns incorporating a hooked breech.

The beauty of some of the newer in-line rifles with a removable breech plug is the fact that at the end of a day in the field, you don't have to shoot the rifle to unload it. The breech plug easily can be unthreaded from the breech end of the barrel and the powder charge and bullet punched out the rear end of the barrel. This is especially handy at the end of a day's hunt in really wet weather. It eliminates having to give the barrel a cleaning and lets you head out next day with a fresh powder charge and confidence the next morning.

The ramrods that come with a rifle are great for an occasional field cleaning or wiping of the bore between shots, but they come with the gun with one purpose primarily in mind -- loading the gun! Anyone really serious about shooting a muzzleloader also should purchase an auxiliary cleaning rod, a rod designed specifically for the task of keeping a muzzleloading rifle's bore spotless. Most of these ramrods are made of stainless steel or some other strong and durable material that can stand up to considerable more use than the gun's standard equipment ramrod. Dixie Gun Works and Tennessee Valley Manufacturing each market a 1/4-inch-diameter stainless steel cleaning rod. It comes complete with a cone-shaped Teflon bore guide that protects the rifling from the abrasive effects of the harder steel. Shooters who put a great deal of powder and lead through their favorite frontloaders also find these rods a better choice for loading when shooting from a bench. By using the metal rods whenever possible, you'll save your frontloader's ramrod for use in the deer woods.

Chapter 10

Hunting The Early Seasons

Most general firearm deer seasons seem to coincide with the peak of the rut, and despite the onslaught of hunters who generally take to the deer woods during these seasons, this still can be a hunter's best time for taking a really good buck with a frontloading rifle. The whitetail hunter who knows how to let other hunters work for him to push a smart ol' buck from its hiding place and in front of a strategically located stand will fill his tag regularly. In areas where deer tend to see little hunting pressure, it's a good bet that a buck will never realize the season is open and will continue following rutting patterns, making even the biggest buck vulnerable.

A study of the special muzzleloading seasons held across the country will reveal that slightly more are held following the general gun seasons than before. Pre-rut early seasons and post-rut late seasons require different hunting tactics. In this chapter we will take a look at hunting those muzzleloader whitetail seasons which fall prior to the general firearms seasons. The following chapter will deal with late season muzzleloading hunts.

Early muzzleloading seasons appeal to different hunters for different reasons. Some like the idea of hunting an early October or November season before the weather turns cold. For others, the early seasons mean getting first shot at the whitetails before they've been pressured by an army of modern-gun-packing hunters which fills the woods for a week or two each fall. While these seasons may give a hunter that first chance at a whitetail buck, the opportunity still doesn't mean that any whitetail buck which is a veteran of several seasons will be a pushover.

Truth is, the pre-rut period can be some of the toughest whitetail hunting of the year. If you are satisfied to tag any whitetail, especially a doe, then filling an early season muzzleloading tag can be relatively easy. However, if you have your sights set on taking a really good buck with your smokepole, you're taking on a real challenge.

The one thing muzzleloading whitetail hunters hunting an early season have in our favor is that we generally have the deer woods practically to ourselves. Food is easy to get at this time of year. A good mast crop has just began to fall, and row crops have matured and may even be under harvest. Living is easy. About the only things on a whitetails buck's mind are eating, snoozing

• The early season is a supreme challenge. Heavier foliage means more cover. Plenty of available food means less deer movement. But the weather generally is warm and we often have the woods almost to ourselves....Photo by Richard P. Smith.

• You'll probably have best early season results by ambushing deer along trails between feeding and bedding areas, or maybe watching water holes. Photo by Gary Clancy.

● .....but there's still something to notice every wrong sound we make. Photo by Richard P. Smith.

and living for the day. Rutting urges are still a month or so away and attempting to pattern a buck at this time of year can cause even veteran whitetail hunters to pull out their hair.

More than once I've located good buck sign in a relatively concentrated area, then spent day after day sitting on stand overlooking some of the most promising looking areas without ever seeing the first glimpse of a good buck. Even when the living is so easy that a whitetail buck may be able to meet all his feeding, watering and bedding needs in less than a hundred yards of travelling, a whitetail's instilled survival instincts may still cause him to do even this small amount of movement under the secrecy of darkness.

I've found my best success in the early season by concentrating on known feeding areas or the trails leading to and from feeding and bedding areas. With such a bounty of foods close at hand, it may be several days before a buck returns to a certain food source, so patience is definitely a must. While a buck may not move far to fill his daily needs, he still moves; the hunter who is in the right place at the right time gets a shot at filling his tag.

The hard core bowhunter who has picked up a muzzleloader to take advantage of the extra hunting season often has a real advantage over the hunter who jumps right in on opening morning of the early muzzleloading seasons. Most bowhunters are notorious for getting a really early start. Few will miss the first couple weeks of the season, which may open as early as late September or early October. As a rule, most archery whitetail seasons open two, three or even four weeks ahead of the early muzzleloading seasons. While the hunting can be even tougher this early in the fall, just being in the deer woods lets the bowhunter establish deer movement patterns before switching to a frontloading rifle.

The smart bowhunter turned black powder burner won't drastically change his hunting tactics simply because he's picked up an arm which triples or quadruples his effective shooting range. Most shots at this time of year generally will be at relatively close range, usually well under 50 yards, primarily because of the foliage still on the trees and underbrush.

This isn't to say that a hunter won't get a hundred-yard or longer shot during a pre-rut whitetail hunt. When you're hunting the edges of a recently harvested cornfield or hay field, an early morning or late evening hunt could call for stretching a shot out past a hundred yards. The farther north an early season hunt is held, the more apt a hunter is to find whitetails feeding in fields, especially where the hardwoods have given way to conifers and non-mast-producing soft hardwoods.

However, in most prime whitetail country, the deer will show a real preference for white oak acorns over just about every other food source. When a good mast crop covers the forest floor with a blanket of acorns, whitetails may never leave the hardwoods for open fields. Even if they do elect to supplement their acorn diet with a little clover, soybeans or corn, more often than not it's well after dark when they do so. Knowing an area is loaded with deer but never seeing the wary whitetails can make for a frustrating hunt. Instead of waiting for the deer to move out into the open, you may have to ease in and hunt the limited range of pre-rut whitetails.

Several years ago I had the privilege of hunting a 13,000-acre farm in western Kentucky during that state's mid-October early muzzleloading deer season. Never before had I hunted a piece of property so loaded with whitetails. The first evening of the hunt the property manager drove me around the farm's miles and miles of field roads. Hundreds of deer were everywhere. Hardly a chopped silage field or hayfield failed to hold 20...30...40 whitetails. Four special hunts on this farm each fall saw some 400 hunters taking nearly 800 deer. On top of this, the farm manager and hired hands had to fill 200 to 300 depredation permits each fall just to keep the growing deer herd somewhat in check.

Still, I knew I was in for a challenging hunt even before I hit the woods the next morning. The weather had turned unusually hot and dry. For several days prior to the opener of the first two-day hunt of the year on the farm, the daytime temperature

• *When crop fields are harvested, food and cover are reduced. How will the deer in your area adapt? You need to know. Photo by Gary Clancy.*

• *For one thing, with crop cover gone, whitetails will make more use of grassy swales and patches of weeds everywhere....the areas we consider as secondary cover and thus so often overlook. Photo by Gary Clancy.*

had jumped into the 90s. It hadn't rained in nearly a month.

My first morning stand was situated along a narrow strip of trees which separated a chopped silage field and a recently cut and baled alfalfa field. The evening before, we had seen nearly a hundred whitetails in two fields. Just to the east of my stand site ran a long hardwood ridge that ended in a steep bluff overlooking a shallow, slow running river. To the west were several small 20 to 40 acre woodlots and more fields like the two I could watch from my stand. I felt confident the deer were bedding along the ridge and had placed my stand to intercept deer coming from the more distant fields.

The trouble was, the whitetails were already well out of the fields before the first hint of daybreak. By nine o'clock, I had seen two small does. While I was sharing the huge farm with nearly a hundred other hunters, I heard fewer than two dozen shots that morning.

With only two days to fill the doe and buck tag I had been issued for the hunt, I quickly realized I needed to find a more promising stand location. Deer sign was everywhere I looked. Tracks upon tracks and fresh droppings everywhere. However, most tracks seemed to be headed to and from the long hardwood ridge. Working the ridgetop toward the river, I jumped quite a few deer as I neared the waterway. The closer I got to the water, the more deer I heard scurrying away through the thick undergrowth.

The river was still nearly half a mile away. Instead of walking all the way to the end of the ridge and spooking all the whitetails, I decided to head back, get my portable climbing stand, find a good tree near the spot where I stopped, then leave the area until just before evening. There was no reason to try getting a shot at fleeing deer in the thick growth, and they certainly weren't going to move far through the middle of the day. I was out of the woods by noon.

I was sitting in the stand about 20 feet off the ground by 4 o'clock that afternoon. Sunset was about 6:30, and I knew I probably would have about a two hour wait before I could expect to see deer. That's exactly the way the hunt went.

About a quarter to six, the woods came

alive with whitetails. More than a dozen does and yearling fawns browsed through the growth below. Several times I caught a glimpse of a small buck, but he wasn't anything I wanted to tag. Several times I thought about filling my doe tag, but decided to wait until I had my buck on the ground.

Suddenly three racks appeared, easing through head high brush. None were trophy class bucks, but I'd decided to settle on the first decent buck I spotted just to get my first hunt of the season off to a successful start. I'd turned the 3X-9X scope aboard my .50-caliber stainless steel rifle to its lowest setting and easily found the bucks in the scope. The trio appeared to be 1-1/2 year-old eight- pointers. They looked like triplets. As soon as the first buck stepped into an opening, I settled the crosshairs just to the rear of the front shoulder and cleanly dropped him in his tracks.

Deer scattered from the brush in every direction, appearing from out of nowhere and flashing white flags as they ran helter skelter through the maturing second growth hardwoods. Not knowing exactly what they were running from, several of the does stopped after running just 40 or 50 yards and within five minutes were back to feeding on freshly fallen acorns.

Very slowly, I eased a pre-measured powder charge from my shirt pocket, snapped the cap from the plastic tube and poured the 100 grain charge of Pyrodex "Select" into the muzzle. Using the palm of my hand, I pushed another saboted bullet into the muzzle of the rifle, eased the ramrod from the stock and shoved the bullet and sabot down over the powder charge. With the ramrod back in place under the barrel, I quickly slipped a percussion cap on the nipple and was ready to shoot again.

A big doe 60 yards away still nervously looked around. Through the scope I could clearly see her head and neck. Many hunters would have taken the shot, actually preferring to shoot a doe in the head or neck to keep from ruining edible meat. Still, I prefer going for the heart and lung area, which offers a much larger kill zone and thus a higher-percentage shot.

Patience finally paid off. Just as the sun dropped below the horizon, the doe eased forward a few yards, offering the clear shot I needed. Again, the jacketed, 260-grain hollow-point did its job. Both my tags were filled. While the buck was one of the smaller whitetails I've taken with muzzleloader, I still felt a real sense of accomplishment in overcoming the hunting conditions and succeed-

• When acorns, especially white oak acorns, start dropping in abundance, you had better know when and where just as soon as the deer, because for a while not much else will matter to the deer. Photo by Richard P. Smith

• With a portable tree stand, you're mobile in the best way — across the ground and up the trees. You can adapt quickly to whatever your scouting tells you to do, and as tough as early season hunting can be, you need to keep your hunting eyes and brain open, looking for what's there instead of just what you want to see. Photo by Tom Fegely.

ing. Plus, with these two deer for the freezer, I could now hunt the next two or three whitetail hunts saving my tag for a trophy class buck.

Occasionally an early muzzleloading season may run right up until the traditional start of the rut. In Saskatchewan the muzzleloading season has grown quickly in popularity. Many big buck hunters now know that this season can be their best chance at taking one of the huge, heavy antlered whitetails which have made this Canadian province famous.

Here, the general firearm season traditionally opens the second week of November, which also normally coincides with the peak of the rut. In this far northern stretch of farm country, winter can come early and despite what you may hear from some sources, unusually cold weather can trigger the start of the rut a week or two early. During a fall of unseasonably cold weather, the rut in this and neighboring provinces can occur anywhere from the third week of October right up until mid-November. The muzzleloading season here is an early one, running through the month of October and right up until the opener of the general firearm season.

When the rut is running a week early, black powder hunters here cash in on the best hunting of the year, and with the least amount of hunting pressure. Some mighty impressive trophy bucks, including many Boone & Crockett record book bucks, are taken each fall during the Saskatchewan muzzleloading season, whether the rut is early or not. For the travelling whitetail hunter from the States, planning a frontloader hunt for Saskatchewan whitetails can be something of a gamble. When conditions are ideal and the rut kicks in early, a hunt here can be a dream come true. On the other hand, if the rut runs late or even if it hits its traditional time window, the early muzzleloading season here can be just as tough as an early season anywhere.

There really are no short cuts or hot tactics to insure that an early muzzleloading season will be productive. If you are already a successful bowhunter, then simply use the same tactics you use when bowhunting the pre-rut. If you're not a bowhunter, it's time you learn some of the techniques and tac-

Early Seasons

tics archers rely on to get close enough to take whitetails at 20 to 30 yards with their limited range equipment.

As a rule, whitetails don't travel great distances at this time of year, which means you will have to learn how to intercept their limited movement patterns. This also means you'll often need to locate your stand closer to where the whitetails may be bedding, which increases the chances of spooking the deer from the area. Your own scent becomes your greatest handicap. Extra care must be taken to position your stand so the air currents work in your favor, carrying your scent away from the hunt area. Also, knee high rubber boots can help prevent leaving scent as you walk to and from your stand.

During early season hunts, I tend to stay away from scent type lures, especially the doe-in-heat or buck-in-rut scents. Instead, I spend a great deal more effort in working to eliminate my odor and take extra care to avoid picking up foreign odors on my clothing and equipment. When I do use a natural scent, it is always a simple whitetail urine which I place in a spray atomizer bottle. A few squirts of this as I walk in and then around my stand leaves a natural deer smell which doesn't necessarily attract whitetails, but which tends to calm them and assure the deer that all is well.

More and more states are now offering both an early and a late muzzleloading whitetail season. Where I have a choice, I'll always take the late season over the early hunt, and in the following chapter you'll learn why. However, if the early hunt is all that's available, I still welcome the challenge.

Chapter 11

Hunting The Late Seasons

As we've already seen in the preceding chapter, hunting a truly trophy class whitetail buck during the early muzzleloader seasons can be anything but easy. The same can pretty well be said for the late season hunts which usually take place during the post-rut period.

Still, those seasons which follow the general firearm hunts remain some of my favorites. First, **they often are the most under-hunted.** The army of orange-coated centerfire-toting whitetail hunters have left the woods and are spending their free time living up to holiday commitments or watching football on television. However, for the knowledgeable whitetail hunter who just isn't ready to hang it up for the year, the late muzzleloader seasons in many states can be extremely productive. The key is to spend enough time in the woods to learn where to find whitetails.

Throughout most whitetail country, the weather can be unpredictable through the month of December and into early January. In the South, this can be a rainy period as warmer Gulf air pushes northward, while throughout most of the North winter has set in. Keep in mind that the farther south you hunt, the later the peak of the rut. In the deep South, December and January can offer some of the best hunting of the year.

The bitter cold temperatures and deep snows of the North and upper Midwest can dictate where a hunter should look for whitetails. The rut has wound down and a whitetail's thoughts have turned back to survival. While does normally come through the breeding period in pretty good condition, many bucks have lost much needed body weight and thoughts turn to food once more.

This isn't to say that the rut comes to an immediate and abrupt stop on any given day or in any given week. Not all does enter the first estrus period at the same time, and a couple of weeks' span from the earliest to the latest doe to come into heat will keep an old buck running from woodlot to woodlot. Where the buck-to-doe ratio is really lopsided, as it is in most whitetail country, there may be only one mature buck for every 10 to 15 does. Quite a few does come out of the primary rut without having been bred.

These same does will once again enter estrus about 30 days later. This period generally is referred to as the "secondary" rut. In the North, upper Midwest and upper

• Depending upon where you're hunting, the late black powder season could put you in the secondary rut, or still in the main rut. This buck was following a doe through a Montana field. Photo by Richard P. Smith.

East Coast, the secondary rut takes place about the same time as many late muzzleloader seasons.

In northern Missouri where I live and do most of my whitetail hunting, the late muzzleloader season overlaps this period perfectly. While game officials claim that the general firearms season in this state actually affects the primary rut very little, I have noticed definite increased rut activity in the area near my home through December. I live only a few miles south of the Iowa state line. Here, the primary rut generally kicks in about the end of the first week of November. Missouri's statewide firearms deer season traditionally opens the second Saturday of the month, with the nine-day season coinciding with the peak of the rut. Nearly a half million gun tags are issued, and for those nine days the hardwoods of the Show-Me state are dotted with fluorescent orange. Most good bucks are taken during this period by smart hunters who have located their stand along an escape route to intercept pressured whitetails headed for less congested territory. When this number of hunters suddenly show up in the deer woods for even such a short period, it has to disrupt breeding activity, even if just a little. Where I live, it seems that much of this rutting activity is now taking place during the secondary rut.

The Missouri late muzzleloading season takes place during early December, two to three weeks after the close of the general firearm season. The "down time" between the two seasons gives the whitetail plenty of time to settle back down and return to more normal routines. With the much, much smaller number of hunters taking to the woods for the muzzleloader season, the deer really don't feel a renewed hunting pressure.

A couple of seasons back, I returned to bowhunting the weekend following the close of the firearm season. There was still considerable rut activity and a number of scrapes near a few of my favorite stands were being hit regularly. Over the course of the three weekends following the gun season, I saw a number of good bucks but failed to get a shot at anything. So when the state's statewide muzzleloader season opened on the first weekend of December,

• Winter cornfields, picked or unpicked, offer great late season hunting. You can stillhunt across them, stand near them, or stand back on an approach trail.

I headed right back to one of those stands with my .50 caliber rifle in hand instead of my compound bow.

That week, the area had experienced its first hard freeze. Opening morning of the muzzleloader season saw temperatures right at 15 degrees. Deer moved all morning, but nothing with antlers showed. About 9:30 I was ready to leave my stand to do a little stillhunting. It had been nearly 45 minutes since I'd spotted my last deer. Even though it was opening morning of the season, I knew I had the woods to myself. I hadn't heard a single shot.

My stand was located in a wide, shallow valley dotted with half-acre grassy openings interspersed with woodlots of about the same size. On each side of the valley, hardwood ridges stretched nearly a mile back to the country gravel road where I had parked in the pre-dawn darkness. In the other direction, the valley opened to an 80-acre cornfield which bordered a small river.

Half the cornfield had been picked before a short rainy period in mid-November had stopped the harvest. I knew the deer were feeding on the corn and had positioned my stand to take advantage of any movement to the field, plus still be able to hunt an active line of rubs and scrapes. As I said, I was about to leave my stand when suddenly deer were moving again. From about 9:30 until about 10:30, more than 20 deer filtered past my stand, all coming from the direction of the cornfield and headed back into the huge stand of hardwoods surrounding my valley.

Shortly after 11:00, two adult does and three yearlings came easing up through one of the small clearings, headed directly to-

Late Seasons

• *With the rut winding down and not much hunting pressure, deer begin bunching up in snow country, staying as close as they safely can to their food supply to conserve energy. Photo by Richard P. Smith.*

ward my stand. Right on their tails, literally, was a fair eight-pointer. Since I was leaving for another muzzleloader hunt in Nebraska in a few days, I decided to take the buck if I got the shot. He gave me a perfect opportunity as he walked past broadside at about 30 yards. The hollow-point put the deer down on the spot.

Next morning, I returned to the same stand, this time with my bow. While the archery deer season shuts down for the regular firearm season in Missouri, bowhunters and muzzleloading hunters can hunt at the same time during the late muzzleloader season, and for the most part neither realizes the other is in the woods. About 10:00, the temperature had warmed to 30 degrees. Without any hint of a breeze, it was an ideal deer hunting morning. As the day before, deer moved all morning, then seemed to quit about 9:00, then picked back up about an hour later. Several small six-pointers had tempted me into drawing on them, mostly to see if I could get away with it, but I hadn't taken a shot.

As if almost a repeat performance of the previous morning, another eight-pointer almost identical to the one I had dropped with a muzzleloader came following a doe right past my stand. An easy 20-yard shot allowed me to fill my first bow tag of the season.

The location of this stand had been particularly good for two reasons. First, because it allowed me effectively to cover the scrape line which was being hit regularly, even though the peak of the rut had been nearly three weeks earlier. Second, because the stand allowed me to cover the movement pattern of whitetails going from the hardwood ridges to the partially harvested cornfields.

During the earlier gun season my friend Brent Hunt also had taken a nice eight-pointer from the same stand. Brent's buck definitely had been in full rut. Before pulling the trigger on the whitetail, he had watched it hit two scrapes, and it was headed for a third when he dropped the deer at 50 yards. Whether my two bucks were still looking to breed does which may have been coming into heat late, or which may have been coming into estrus for a second time, I really can't say. However, both definitely were still rutting.

While the second rut period can provide great whitetail action, especially where hunting pressure is practically nonexistent during a late muzzleloader season, rut patterns definitely begin to taper off quickly as

• Cattails, other marshland, CRP fields, weedy draws....all will hide deer any time but especially so when hunting pressure pushes them out of the woods and other areas more-heavily hunted. Photo by Gary Clancy.

the year begins to wind down. By mid December, deer in the northern zones have begun to bunch together and survival becomes their primary concern. At this time of year most whitetail movements center around their primary food source.

This isn't to say that you can expect a big buck to be standing around just about any cornfield or along any acorn-covered hardwood ridge. However, if the weather has turned cold and harsh, these spots are great places to start looking.

The late muzzleloading season in Iowa is without a doubt my favorite black powder hunt of the year .... provided I'm lucky enough to be drawn for one of the limited number of non-resident tags. The southern portion of this state is as fine of big buck country as you'll find anywhere on the North American continent -- Mexico, the United States or Canada. Traditionally, this season opens just before Christmas and runs into the second week of January. If you've ever been in Iowa at this time of year, you know how cold and windy it can get. I've actually hunted when the wind chill factor was pushing 60 degrees below zero.

However, when it turns that cold, deer have to feed to generate the body heat needed to keep from freezing to death. While you're not likely to see a big buck throw all caution to the wind and gluttonously fill his stomach with corn right in broad daylight, you can narrow down your search for whitetails by concentrating your efforts on known feeding areas. It's a good bet the deer won't be all that far away.

Deer in this state are pressured pretty hard during the general gun season, both of which take place in early December. A favorite tactic in Iowa is to drive deer from the broken woodlots and brushy draws. Here, during the general gun season, party hunting is allowed, which for those of you who aren't familiar with the term, means that every member of the hunting party can keep on hunting to help others in the hunting party fill their tags. Drives with 20 to 30 hunters are common. As you might imagine, the deer are continuously pushed from the

• Bales in hayfield make great blinds, and brushy field edges can harbor bedded whitetails or serve as pathways of cover for deer to move along. Late season conditions will vary with latitude and weather, but if there's no rut going on, just figure on food. The deer are, too. Top photos by Gary Clancy.

sparse cover.

With so much hunting pressure, even if for just a short period, the whitetails become nocturnal, feeding almost entirely at night. Only a day or two separate the last day of the modern (shotgun) gun season from the opener of the late muzzleloading season, and the bucks you find yourself hunting are extremely reclusive. Still, the late muzzleloader season in Iowa remains one of my favorites.

For several months, most of my hunting has been totally based on proper stand placement and having the patience to stick with the stand long enough to be in it when the deer move. Rarely will I spend much time in a stand when hunting the late season in the Hawkeye state. Instead, I spend most of my time slowly stillhunting through 20- to 30-acre woodlots or along grassy and brushy draws which border a cornfield. The latter is actually one of the best places to look for deer at this time of year. I particularly like to hunt small grassy or weedy depressions which are almost totally surrounded by a harvested grain field. Deer don't like to move far from their food source when the temperature dips below zero, and as long as a shallow depression or ditch bank, pond dam, or even a brushy fence row provides a break from the wind, deer will use it for cover. Sometimes these areas are so out in the open that just getting close to them before the deer break can be a real problem.

Farm country such as that where I hunt in Iowa can be extremely open, and shots can push the outermost effective limits of a muzzleloading rifle. Fortunately, this state allows the use of a telescopic sight. Despite what many traditional muzzleloading shooters feel about optics aboard a frontloading rifle, a scope will make a much better shot out of anyone once the shots are out at 100 to 150 yards.

The colder the weather, the more difficult it is for equipment to function properly. Muzzleloading rifles are certainly no exception. When temperatures drop below zero, the mechanics of a muzzleloading rifle which worked so smoothly in warmer weather may not want to function at all.

Many black powder hunters try to cold-

● *Tree stands can be iceboxes in late season, so consider staying on the ground with a ground blind, or stillhunting when conditions are right. The author prefers stillhunting on his December Midwest-state hunts. Photo by Gary Clancy.*

• What do you do for your rifle in super-cold weather? Keep it dry and free of sticky oil or grease. Bare metal or an exremely light oiling is best. Photo by Richard P. Smith.

weatherize the lock, trigger and any other moving mechanical part of the rifle by liberally applying oil or a lithium/graphite-based grease. More often than not, this only creates greater problems. After more than 30 whitetail seasons hunting with a muzzleloader, some much colder than I care to remember, I've discovered the best thing I can do to help insure that the lock or trigger mechanism will function properly in extremely cold weather is, believe it or not, NOTHING! Well, okay, almost nothing.

Any time oil or grease is applied, extremely cold temperatures either can make the metal surfaces become sticky or, in the case of a heavy-based grease, can cause that grease to form a thick, caked surface. While either will protect the metal surfaces from rusting or corrosion, neither actually does a good job of lubricating precision fitting parts for freer, easier-moving performance. The precise fit of a muzzleloader's lock requires a number of polished bearing surfaces for smooth operation. Once these surfaces become coated with a sticky oil or grease, a lock actually becomes more sluggish.

One of the coldest whitetail hunts I've been on took place in southeastern Minnesota. That hunt was during the general firearm season instead of a late muzzleloader season, but the weather encountered was more appropriate for a late, late hunt instead of early November.

A cold Arctic front had pushed down out of Canada, sending temperatures well below zero and dropping nearly a foot of snow on the ground. By the time I arrived in hunting camp a couple of days before the season opener, there were nearly 15 inches of snow on the ground and early morning temperatures hovered right at 10 to 15 degrees below zero. Weather forecasts called for more of the same.

The snow sure made it easy to find fresh sign. After a full day of scouting, I had located the perfect spot to position my climbing tree stand. A long hardwood ridge about a half-mile from camp was topped with a cornfield nearly a mile in length and nearly 200 yards across in most places ... except one. Here, the field narrowed to about 100 yards. A deep, brushy draw cut into the field from one side, forming a narrow spot where I felt a wary old buck would choose to cross the open expanse.

I was hunting the boundary of a privately owned 1,800 acre farm. On the farm itself, I knew of seven other hunters but didn't feel they would be placing much pressure on the whitetails. However, directly behind me was a huge 3,000 acre tract of public hunting land, and I was at the back edge of the property. I knew the area would see considerable hunting pressure and realized that if I could stick with my stand long enough, sooner or later a good buck would be pushed across the ridgetop into the less pressured private property. The funnel created by the brushy draw cutting into the field from the opposite side seemed to be the most logical crossing point. I positioned my stand so I could look down into the bowl formed by the draw, yet cover the entire expanse of the crossing point.

The first morning of the hunt was uneventful. All morning long, deer crossed the narrow spot in the field, most going from the public hunting side of the ridge over to the privately-owned side. Except for two mediocre 120-class bucks, all the other two dozen or so whitetails which crossed that morning were antlerless. The cold minus-10 temperature forced me to give up the stand by ten o'clock, but after a hot lunch and sharing a few hunting stories with several other hunters in camp, I was back in my stand and stuck it out until dark. The afternoon hunt was pretty well a repeat of the morning -- plenty of deer, but none of the huge bucks this region of southeastern Minnesota is noted for producing.

A fresh snow was falling as I left camp in the pre-dawn darkness the next morning. The temperature was a cold minus-14, and with the stiff breeze the wind-chill was somewhere around minus-30 degrees. To keep from building up a sweat during the half-mile walk through the deep snow and the climb up the side of the steep Mississippi River-country ridge, I elected to wear only a light Polar Fleece jacket and pants over wool underwear. In a knapsack I carried a heavy, insulated four-in-one parka and matching pants, plus a pair of 100 percent wool trousers. These I would slip on once I reach my stand and cooled down.

• *Good scouting homework will have you in the right position when pressured bucks head for cover. Photo by Tom Fegely.*

A wool face mask and an old wool blanket wrapped around my insulated boots made sitting in the stand much easier than the previous morning, despite the fact that it was a few degrees colder. I knew it would be hard for other hunters to stay with their stands, and once they began moving around they would keep deer on the move. The longer I could stay with my stand the better the chances of a good buck crossing within range of my muzzleloader.

Despite the low temperatures, snow continued to fall throughout the morning. A half-dozen times whitetails would seem suddenly to appear from out of nowhere, and I would lift the rifle from my lap, dust off the light layer of snow and get ready, just in case a buck was to show. That finally happened around 9:30.

Eight does had appeared on my side of the field, about a hundred yards to my left. Nervously, the whitetails milled around, then headed for the brushy draw coming in from the other side. As I had done several times that morning, I shook the snow from the rifle and waited for a buck to appear.

A good eight-pointer joined the does as they eased across the field, and I followed his movement through the scope, cranked up to its highest (10X) setting. I'd decided to wait until the deer reached the lower side of the field before taking the shot. Every deer which had crossed the field always stopped on the opposite side before disappearing into the brush. There wasn't any reason to believe these deer would do anything differently. I would rather take a shot at a motionless target than one which was moving through deep snow with a rocking horse movement.

The deer did just as I had hoped and stopped to mill around. A doe standing directly behind the buck kept me from taking the shot. I kept the crosshairs of the scope just to the rear of the deer's shoulder, waiting for the opportunity. Suddenly it dawned

• A scrape made in snow is even more dramatic than when there's just bare dirt tossed around, and a sure sign that late season bucks are still on the prod. Photo by Gary Clancy.

• It's not only the hardware that has trouble with top quality performance in cold weather. When we're warm, we sit more quietly, have more patience, hunt more positively and definitely enjoy it more. Sometimes, though — like about 4 p.m. on a cold, gray winter afternoon — we have every right to wonder just how much more of this fun we can stand. Photo by Richard P. Smith.

on me that all nine deer were looking back across the field in the direction from which they had just come. I leaned forward in the stand and looked back in that direction. There stood one of the finest ten-pointers I've ever seen.

As the deer along the opposite side of the field slowly filtered into the fringe cover of the draw, the big ten-pointer moved across the field to join them. I was tempted to take a shot at the buck as it moved across the open about 130 yards away, but once again I held off, hoping it too would stop along the opposite side and offer a standing target. Once again, the deer did just what I hoped.

My rifle had been sighted to print about three inches high at 100 yards, which would put the saboted bullet dead on at about 130 yards. I guessed the buck to be right at that, so I held dead on for a spot just to the rear of the front shoulder. I slipped off the safety, steadied my hold by resting the rifle against the trunk of the tree, and eased back on the trigger. I heard the big jacketed hollow-point drive home and watched as the buck nose-dived into the snow. The big 160-score whitetail was down for the count.

Prior to this hunt, I had taken my rifle apart to remove excess oil from every internal part. The plunger style hammer and inside of the receiver had been sprayed with a good cleaner/degreaser to remove all traces of oil. Then, the metal surfaces were wiped with a cloth which had been lightly sprayed with "3-in-1" oil. Despite the bitter cold, the rifle performed flawlessly. I noticed absolutely no drag on the hammer as it fell, and the bullet went exactly where I wanted it to.

Over the years, I've hunted with just about every kind of muzzleloader imaginable. Extremely cold weather is a test of any equipment. When time is taken to remove excess oil from internal surfaces, your rifle will function better whether it's a traditionally styled side-hammer or modern percussion in-line rifle.

Likewise, extremely cold weather can affect how you load your rifle. Projectiles just seem to fit more snugly, and the cold definitely will reduce your ability to feel how much pressure you're putting on the ramrod. Getting consistent performance from your hunting loads can be a little more difficult than during warmer weather. Always do some shooting under cold weather conditions to see how your rifle and loads perform before investing the time to try to locate a late season whitetail buck.

• *The sweet smile of success doesn't need any words.*

Chapter 12

The Muzzleloading Alternative

Hunting whitetails with a muzzleloader continues to be one of today's fastest growing shooting and hunting sports. The popularity of hunting deer with a slow-to-load frontloader can be largely attributed to the bonus hunting opportunities provided by the special muzzleloading seasons as today's whitetail herds continue to grow.

Today's muzzleloading hunter is not out there to play Daniel Boone, he's out there to hunt deer and wants to pack the most efficient muzzleloader the law will allow. A few of these rifles are so accurate and effective that a growing number of serious whitetail hunters are turning to the single-shot black powder rifles where they are allowed to pack a muzzleloader as an alternative hunting arm in shotgun areas.

As this was written, whitetail hunters in nine states were required to use shotguns for hunting whitetail during the general firearm season. This is nine states where no centerfire rifles can be used at all. Hunters in another 11 states were also required to use a modern smoothbore in as much as half of their home state. In all, as many as five million whitetail hunters may be required to rely on a shotgun loaded with rifled or saboted slugs. (A few states allow the use of buckshot.) In all 20 of these shotgun states or states with significant shotgun zones, a muzzleloading rifle can be used as an option.

Where population densities are so great to make the use of centerfire rifles unsafe, the limited range of a shotgun and slug is ideal. But then, so is the limited range and especially the single-shot aspect of a muzzleloading rifle. Many hunters are turning to the muzzleloading deer rifle because it is consistently more accurate than slug guns, rifled or smoothbore, and the frontloaders extend their range slightly.
It doesn't take a rocket scientist to determine that with the proper loads, a top quality muzzleloading rifle can add 50 yards to the effective range of most hunters.

One thing is certain, and that is that the quality and variety of modern shotguns designed for hunting whitetails has gotten considerably better since I first started hunting deer in my home state of Illinois more than 30 years ago. Back then, there were only a couple of true "deer slug" guns on the market, and this was before we started seeing rifling in the bores of some models. In fact, back then Illinois required the use of shotguns and "rifled" slugs (or a

The Alternative

• *A great deal of time and money went into building this custom 12-gauge slug gun. Still, one of the modern in-line percussion muzzleloading rifles will outshoot it past 100 yards.*

muzzleloader). A shotgun with a rifled barrel actually was illegal.

Along with today's improved slug guns we've also seen the introduction of greatly improved slug loads for hunting deer. Some of the effective saboted shotgun slugs have been designed for use with rifled shotgun barrels, and are capable of amazing accuracy out to about a hundred yards, but at that point most begin to lose accuracy and knockdown effectiveness.

To make honest comparisons of today's modern slug guns and slug loads with some of the better quality muzzleloaders now available, I did considerable shooting with a variety of slugs out of the rifled barrel of a scoped Remington 870 slug gun. Remington, Winchester and Federal saboted slugs all turned in acceptable three- to four-inch groups at 100 yards. However, with the Remington sighted dead on at that distance, it was the performance beyond that point which keeps this excellent slug gun and others from being serious 150-yard whitetail guns.

On the average, practically all the slugs which hit on at 100 yards dropped a full 16 to 18 inches at 150 yards. This isn't to say they didn't have sufficient remaining energy to kill a whitetail cleanly. At the muzzle, the Federal slug generates just over 2,000 foot-pounds of energy. At 100 yards, the saboted .50 caliber projectile drives home with around 1,100 foot-pounds of energy, and at 150 yards it's still good for about 1,000 foot-pounds. The ballistics for the Remington and Winchester slugs aren't all that different.

The biggest trouble I see with trying to take a whitetail at 150 yards with a modern shotgun and saboted slug is simply the shooter's inability to place the slug in the kill zone. Most of the groups I fired with all three brands of slugs at 150 yards were wide open eight- to 10-inch groups. Combine this lack of accuracy with nearly a foot and a half of drop and the hunter who takes a 150-yard shot with even a quality slug gun better have Lady Luck on his side.

Unfortunately, only a fraction of the hunters who head out with a slug-loaded shotgun take their deer hunting seriously enough to put together a real shotgun deer hunting rig with a rifled barrel and a good scope aboard. Most tend to use the same scattergun they pack for upland birds or even for waterfowl, simply swapping the shot loads they normally use for rifled or saboted slugs. Even those hunters who spend the time and money to refine a real slug gun for hunting deer normally still rely on a poor "shotgun" trigger. Getting rifle-like accuracy with a shotgun is just a tough thing to do.

There's really only one reason why a modern shotgun hunter would forego the firepower of three to five quick shots with a good semi-auto or pump shotgun to hunt with a single shot muzzleloading black powder rifle. That reason is accuracy, the ability to be able to put that single shot exactly where it needs to go out there at 150 to 175 yards. Several of today's more sophisticated muzzleloading rifles offer that kind of performance.

The load for my muzzleloader doesn't quite match the energy levels produced by the Federal saboted shotgun slug mentioned earlier, but it's more than ample for taking down even a big whitetail buck. At the muzzle, a 100-grain charge of Pyrodex "Select" pushes the saboted, 260-grain, .45-caliber bullet at around 1,600 fps and generates approximately 1,500 foot-pounds of energy. Downrange at a hundred yards, the bullet retains about 1,100 foot-pounds of energy, and out at 150 yards it hits home with more than 800 foot-pounds of energy.

A lot is written about the energy levels needed to insure a clean kill on whitetails; most "experts" agree that 1,000 foot-pounds should be considered the minimum effective energy level. When we're talking about .25 to .30 caliber bullets of 130 to 170 grains, then I agree. However, when we're talking about a larger .44 or .45 caliber pistol bullet of 240 to 300 or so grains, then I think the size of the bullet's striking surface and added weight will more than make up

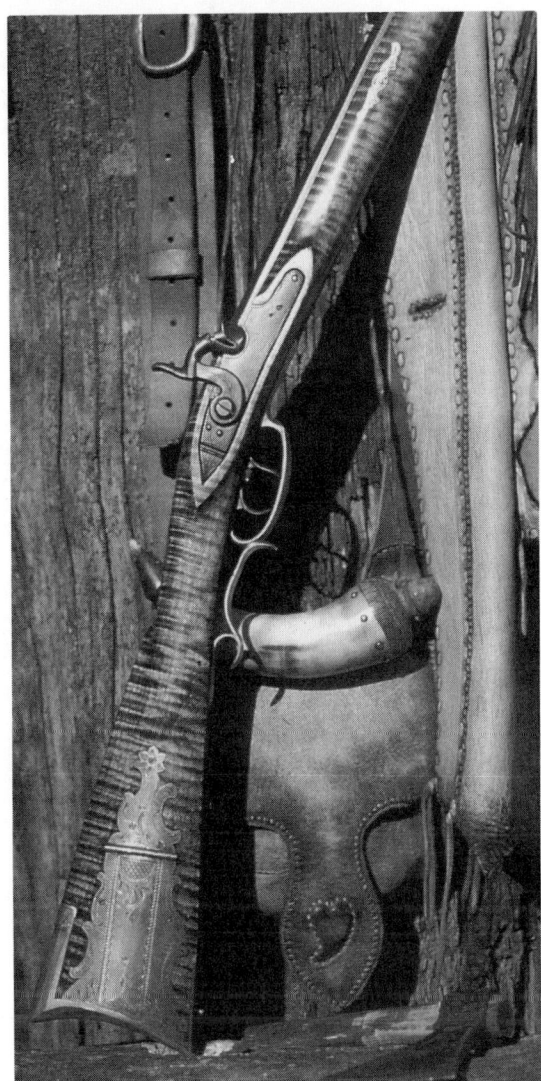

● *As pretty as this well-built custom Kentucky rifle may be, it has been built to shoot a patched round ball and won't give the whitetail hunter any advantage over shooting a modern shotgun with a rifled or saboted slug.*

The Alternative

• The "average" muzzleloading rifle is considerably more accurate than the "average" shotgun loaded with slugs.

for 200 or 300 foot-pounds less energy. Let's take a look at several kills which have been made with my favorite load and see how well the bullet performed.

The longest shot I've made on a whitetail with a muzzleloading rifle was made in Nebraska during that state's general rifle season. In this state, as in about half the states with a muzzleloading season, a scope cannot be used on a rifle when hunted with during the muzzleloader season. However, in all such states a scope is perfectly legal aboard a muzzleloader when it is used during a general rifle or shotgun season.

Prior to the hunt, I had done considerable shooting with my rifle, a .50-caliber MK-85 "Predator", and a variety of saboted bullets. The 260-grain Speer emerged as the most accurate out of my rifle. With one of the Simmons "44 Mag" 3.5X-10X variables mounted on the rifle's receiver, I found it relatively simple to punch 1-1/2 inch groups at 100 yards, and at 150 yards the rifle and load consistently printed groups of about three inches. The rifle was sighted four inches high at 100 yards so it would be closer to being on at 150 yards.

Fortunately, I had used the same rifle earlier in the year for a caribou hunt in Alaska and had put several pounds of powder through it to see just what kind of accuracy I could expect at 200 yards. With the rifle sighted four inches high at 100 yards, it printed about two inches low at 150. At 200, the 260-grain hollow-point hit a good 10 inches below point of aim.

My hunt took place along the Republican River in south-central Nebraska, only about 20 miles north of the Kansas state line. A business meeting allowed me only three days for the hunt. The first two were spent sitting on several different stands, from

• *John Thorpe took this heavy-racked Iowa buck on a short drive.*

which I saw plenty of deer, including a number of bucks. Several were in the 120 to 130 class, but I knew the property well enough to know to hold off for bigger bucks and let these pass. By noon the third day, I was wishing I had taken one of the respectable 10-pointers I had let walk.

The landowner and an old hunting partner of mine who lived in the area volunteered to make a couple of last minute drives for me. The first drive pushed nearly 30 deer right in front of my stand, but none sported antlers. We had time for one last drive before I loaded up and headed home.

I took a stand in a bulldozed pile of brush and stumps at one end of a long, narrow strip of cottonwoods and underbrush which was bordered on one side by the Republican River and by an 80-acre cornfield on the other. My two drivers took their pickup truck and made a half-mile drive to the other end, then began the long slow push through.

A few hundred yards from where I sat waiting, 20 or so does appeared at the edge of the harvested cornfield. They were nervous but for some reason still reluctant to come my way. The deer milled around for four or five minutes, then started across the open field in single file. The last deer to walk out of the brush was a good 10-point buck.

The deer were angling slightly toward me, and if they remained on course, they would pass about 180 yards from where I watched through the 10X scope. Suddenly, the deer stopped and began milling around again. Several more does emerged from the brush at about the same spot where I had first noticed this group of deer as they emerged from the brush at the edge of the field.

The buck was standing facing me at a slight angle as he watched the other deer lope to catch up. The crosshairs of the scope settled somewhere between the white patch on his throat and the top of his back. I'd decided to try to slip the 260 grain bullet between the brisket and the left front shoulder. The angle of the shot would put the bullet into the chest cavity.

I guessed the deer to be nearly 200 yards away. With the crosshairs holding about 10 inches above where I'd like the bullet to hit, I eased back on the trigger. The rifle recoiled lightly and I lost sight of the buck in the scope, but I heard the unmistakable wallop of the bullet. I looked over the scope just in time to see the deer run flat out for 20 yards, then collapse.

That buck was taken at 193 long steps. The bullet caught him perfectly and angled back through the chest cavity, doing considerable damage to heart and lungs. It then proceeded on through the liver and ended up just under the hide of the right rear ham. The recovered bullet was a picture perfect expanded bullet which retained about 90 percent of its original weight. At nearly 200 yards that bullet still had enough steam to penetrate a big whitetail -- 200 pounds, field

> "With the crosshairs about 10 inches above intended impact point, I eased back on the trigger...That buck was taken at 193 long steps."

dressed -- from front to rear.

I've actually found that these bullets tend to punch through more frequently when deer are taken at ranges of a hundred yards or farther. At that distance, the bullets have slowed some and expansion isn't quite as rapid as on closer deer. The big hollow-points often punch out the other side, but exit holes are big enough to show that the bullet did its job. But then, I guess the buck laying less than 40 yards from where it was standing when shot also is evidence the bullet performed well.

When hunting open country, I like to sight my rifle high so I don't have to start calculating when I spot a buck at 150 or 160 yards; but what if a buck suddenly appears at 25 or 30 yards?

If and when I do have to calculate for a shot, it's a lot easier for me to do it on a close target than on a distant target. With my rifle sighted three inches high at 100 yards, it prints the bullet right at 4-1/2 inches high at 50 yards and a little less at 25 yards. If a deer shows at that range, I simply hold just a little lower and take the shot.

Several seasons back I was hunting in west-central Illinois during the second half of that state's split shotgun season. I had sighted my favorite .50 caliber and 260 grain saboted bullets to shoot high at 100 yards, dead on at about 135 yards and a couple of inches low at 150. I was hunting the edge of an open cornfield and honestly expected shots of no less than 100 yards.

I was totally caught off guard when an eight-pointer appeared out of nowhere about 30 yards away in the brush directly behind my stand. Careful to avoid being spotted, I turned the 2X-7X scope down to its lowest magnification, slipped the rifle's safety off and easily found the buck in the scope. I let the crosshairs settle just to the rear of the front shoulder, then lowered my sight picture until I was holding just above the line of white which indicated the bottom of the chest cavity. When the rifle bucked back, that whitetail literally dropped in its tracks. In fact, the deer never even rolled over.

The bullet had caught the big bodied buck squarely through the lungs and heart. Internal damage to organs was tremendous. At such close range, that hollow-point must have reached maximum expansion before ever reaching the inside of the chest cavity. The bullet was recovered under the hide on the opposite side, extremely flattened, chewed up from hitting bone, but still nearly 70 percent intact. That buck was dead before it hit the ground. I'd say the bullet had done an excellent job.

Having grown up in a state where shot-

Chapter 12 - Page 129

● *Muzzleloading offers many hunters a chance to hunt during the prime time of the rut. Calls and grunt tubes then may improve your chances. Photo by John L. Sloan.*

guns have been the only legal modern long gun to use on deer (the state has added a handgun season in recent years), I've been on my share of drives and have seen how slugs perform on whitetails. The big chunks of lead are notorious for punching right through without a good transfer of energy. Seldom will a big buck go down to a single hit, and two or three follow-up shots often are necessary. Some of the saboted slugs now available will do a considerably better job than the old rifled Foster-style slugs that are still used today and which were the most commonly used slug design before the 1980s.

Right out of the box, few of today's shotguns are capable of producing 100-yard hunting accuracy. The vast majority will do well to keep shots inside of five to six inches at 50 yards, and to get any shotgun and slug combination to print a four-inch group out at 100 yards will require a great deal of shooting to determine just which slug is the most compatible to the gun. It's a good bet that to obtain groups at a hundred yards which even come close to four inches, the shotgun will have to have a rifled barrel. If it didn't come with one, then you will be faced with buying one if you want to get the absolute best performance available from a shotgun and slugs.

Building an accurate slug gun can be costly. I know of a few extremely serious whitetail hunters who have upward of $1,500 invested in a shotgun in order to get it to print inside of three to four inches at 100 yards. Still, because of the poor downrange performance of slugs, they're still

The Alternative

packing a gun which, for the most part, is effective only out to about 125 yards. For about half that amount, they could have bought a top-of-the-line rifle, scoped it to get 150- to 160-yard effectiveness, and still had enough left over to pay for an out-of-state hunting trip next fall.

Today's hunter has several well-built percussion in-line rifles to choose from — Modern Muzzleloading's Knight line, Thompson/Center Arms' "Thunder Hawk"; Connecticut Valley Arms Spanish import, the "Apollo"; White Systems' "Super 91" and "Whitetail Series" rifles, and Gonic Arms' "GA-87".

All these rifles will vary some in design. All, however, feature efficient and surefire in-line percussion ignition systems, fast twist rifling from one-turn-in-20 inches to one-turn-in-32 inches for superior accuracy with hard hitting conical bullets or saboted handgun slugs, plus each comes with a receiver that's drilled and tapped for easy installation of a scope. Each of the rifles just mentioned is fully capable of producing 100- to 150-yard performance that will eclipse that of the best modern shotgun and slug loads.

Hunting with a muzzleloader isn't for everyone. No matter how accurate and efficient modern in-line rifles become, there always will be those hunters who will never give up the firepower of quick second and third follow-up shots with a modern pump or semi-auto shotgun. However, if you've grown tired of trying to hunt whitetails with a quail gun, perhaps you should take a closer look at the ultra-modern frontloaders now available. You'll be surprised what you can do with just one shot when you have the ability to put that shot exactly where you want it to go.

Chapter 13

Muzzleloading For Other Big Game

Success with a muzzleloader on whitetails has caused an increasing number of these hunters to look beyond deer, to rely on the guns for hunting additional big game species. In fact, hunting with a muzzleloader has become so popular that hunters are now using the black powder big game rifles for everything from desert bighorn sheep to grizzlies.

Due to the usually open terrain in which some mule deer and all pronghorn antelope are normally hunted, these two species have always been pretty well considered the modern rifleman's game. Shots out to 200 yards are the norm instead of the exception, and today's mule deer and pronghorn hunter has come to rely on flat shooting centerfire rifles to meet the challenge.

So, who would ever consider going after such wary trophies with a muzzleloading rifle? Actually, thousands of hunters do each year, and as surprising as it may seem, their chances of taking a trophy class buck can be considerably better than for most of today's centerfire toting hunters.

There are two reasons. First is the fact that several states now schedule special muzzleloading seasons for pronghorn and mule deer, with these seasons running well ahead of the centerfire seasons for the same areas or hunt units. The number of hunters afield usually is just a fraction of the number of centerfire hunters who may later hunt the same area. The other reason is the effectiveness of today's muzzleloading rifle, especially when loaded with some of the effective modern conical or saboted bullets.

Currently, Wyoming offers the hunter his or her best chance for tagging a pronghorn. Late each summer or early in the fall, the state opens a number of its antelope hunting areas to a muzzleloading season. For all units combined, the number of muzzleloading permits issued amount only to about a thousand. From time to time a hunt for a particular unit may be deemed a "primitive weapons" hunt, permitting the use of archery gear, muzzleloaders or even certain early breechloading black powder rifles, such as the old Sharps, trap-door Springfield and Remington rolling block rifles in such calibers as .45/70, .45/90 or .50/70.

Off and on since the early 1980s, I have taken advantage of these special hunts in Wyoming. I've enjoyed every one, but one sticks in my mind, since I managed to take my first 200 yard big game trophy with a

● *The author built this muzzleloading rifle which would allow him to take big game out past 150 yards. He took this Wyoming pronghorn with a single shot at more than 200 yards.*

muzzleloader.

Primarily for this hunt, I spent the summer building a rifle for that 200-yard shot. The heart of the rifle was one of the custom hunting stocks produced by Reinhart Fajen for the popular Thompson/Center Hawken rifle. From the wrist rearward, this stock is turned the same as a modern center-fire rifle stock, complete with Monte Carlo comb. From the wrist forward, the stock is turned to accept the lock, triggers, breech plug tang, ramrod, trigger guard, nose-cap, wedge plates and the Thompson/Center Hawken barrel.

I was planning to shoot one of the then-brand-new, 410-grain, solid-based, hollow-point Buffalo Bullets and wanted something faster than the one-turn-in-48 inches rate of rifling twist found in the Thompson/Center barrel. I contacted a custom barrelmaker and had him cut me a barrel of the same 15/16-inch diameter with .005-inch deep rifling which spun with a much faster one-turn-in-24 inches. This was breeched with the Thompson/Center breech and fitted with all the other hardware needed to drop right into the Fajen stock.

I replaced the standard open Hawken sights with a base for one of the long-eye-relief handgun scopes, primarily to get away from the side-hammer lock mechanism and the fouling which usually smuts up the barrel and any scope which may have been mounted close to the breech end of the barrel.

After considerable shooting, I discovered I could print the big Buffalo Bullet inside three inches at 100 yards consistently when shooting 100 grains of FFg black powder. However, with a slightly lighter 90-grain charge, the rifle would print inside 2-1/2 inches consistently. That's the charge I settled on.

I met up with a number of old hunting buddies from Utah, Indiana, Colorado and Tennessee in an area about a hundred miles north of Rocks Springs, Wyoming. All were hardcore traditionalists. In fact, several were hunting their antelope with long barreled flintlock rifles of authentic pre-1800 design. The sight of my modern muzzleloading rig sent them reeling!

The rifle had been sighted to print the 410-grain Buffalo Bullet dead on at 150

• *Outdoor writer Tom Fegely took this pronghorn at nearly 150 yards with a Knight MK-85 Knight Hawk.*

yards, which meant it was a good seven inches high at 100 yards, and nine inches low at 200 yards. For the first couple of mornings, I watched several good bucks work along a low ridge about a mile from camp. Each day, they followed basically the same route, passing within a couple hundred yards of a small rise.

Before daylight the next morning, I was snuggled into a shallow depression I had scooped out in a horseshoe-shaped clump of sagebrush on the top of that rise. All morning long, antelope passed within easy range of the muzzleloader, including several tempting 14-inch bucks. Then, just after noon, two real trophy bucks came working along the side of the ridge. I guessed the antelope to be about 225 yards and held my horizontal crosshair right along the back of the biggest of the two. At the shot, the pronghorn disappeared. The heavy conical had caught the record book, 15-1/2-inch buck perfectly and anchored him on the spot...at 240 yards! I paced it off.

I don't promote such long range riflery for everyone. But anyone who takes the time to work up his load and gets to know his rifle's 200-yard capability will discover that it will do the job. Today, anyone looking to rework a Thompson/Center Hawken into a serious hunting rifle as I did will find the task a lot easier. Fajen still offers this stock and the Green Mountain Rifle Barrel Company now offers a drop-in replacement barrel for the Hawken known as their "Long Range Hunter" which features a fast one-turn-in-28 inches rate of rifling twist, and comes with the breech, tenon and ramrod thimble already installed. The barrel can be installed on any Thompson/Center Hawken rifle in a matter of minutes.

Little did I know then that the rifle I built for that hunt, and which I wrote about a lot during the mid 1980s, would become the basis for many of today's modernistic muzzleloading hunting rifles. There are a number of exceptional rifles now available right off a dealer's gun rack which will outperform my custom rig.

More recently, I made a trip to north central Wyoming with Tom Fegely, an outdoor writer friend. Tom had used his Knight

Hawk to take several whitetails in the East and Midwest but had never really had the opportunity to take a shot past 100 yards. My goal was to get Tom into a situation where he would have to shoot at ranges of 130 to 150 yards.

We spent the first couple of days in a remote region of the Powder River breaks looking for trophy mule deer. We had spotted a number of good 4x4 bucks, but nothing to get excited about. Tom had only two more days to hunt, so we decided to concentrate on trying to find him a pronghorn which would meet the minimum score of 63 Boone & Crockett points to qualify for the muzzleloading record book.

We teamed up with another old hunting partner of mine, Ted Schumacher, of Lake DeSmet, Wyoming. Ted operates Lone Wolf Outfitters and is one of the most respected trophy antelope guides in north central Wyoming. He had us looking at 14-1/2 to 15-inch bucks within an hour.

When Tom had arrived in Wyoming, we first spent several hours on the range to resight the rifle for the wide open country of the Powder River Badlands. Tom decided to try the same load which performed so well in the .50-caliber MK-85 Grand American rifle I would later use on mule deer. It took a few rounds to get his .50 caliber rifle to print the hollow-point four inches high at 100 yards. With the 100-grain charge of Pyrodex "Select" he was shooting, that bullet would drop six inches at 150 yards, allowing him to hold dead on out to that range.

When the opportunity came, that's exactly what he did. Using an old abandoned ranch out-building for cover, Tom managed to slip within 150 yards of a good buck that was chasing does. Using the building as a rest, he held dead on the buck's rib cage and squeezed off the shot. The bullet flew true; the buck went only 20 yards and piled up. The pronghorn would score well into the upper 60s.

A couple of hours later, Tom decided to go for a 4x4 mule deer we had spotted. His stalk got him to within 150 yards of the buck before it decided to leave its bed. Holding exactly as he had for the pronghorn, he dropped his second 150-yard muzzleloading trophy of the afternoon.

My chance at a good mule deer buck came several days after Tom had left for home. Ted and I had looked over more than a hundred bucks in just two days. A couple had tempted me, but I was determined to take a healthy 4x4 that I knew would make the muzzleloading record book with room to spare.

We were headed for another of Ted's hunting areas when we spotted three really good bucks travelling together. From the vehicle we watched the trio continue on across open country for several miles, finally crossing onto property where Ted had permission to hunt. Eventually, the deer moved into a deep wash and stayed there. It was mid-day and our guess was that they had bedded.

A one-mile stalk brought me to within 150 yards of where I had last seen the three big mule deer. I slowly eased up on the high point of a low ridge adjacent to the draw and immediately spotted antler tips. One of the bucks caught my movement and stood. The next thing I knew, all three bucks were standing broadside on a small point where the wash branched.

The deer were all good, any of which would qualify for the muzzleloading record book. I gave them all the once-over through the scope and settled on the rear buck. He seemed to be the largest of the three.

From the kneeling position, I held dead center of his chest cavity, slipped the side safety off, took a breath, released half of it, then began the gentle squeeze on the trigger. The Timney featherweight trigger broke crisp and clean. The rifle bucked back lightly and when the muzzle dropped back down, the buck was nowhere in sight.

The hollow-point had caught the deer perfectly, knocking it back into the wash, where it was down for the count. That's the kind of performance I like from a muzzleloading big game rifle.

Whether you have your sights set on antelope or mule deer, you need to be ready for long range shooting. Shots of 100 to 150 yards often require a good stalk. Such ranges will definitely test the effectiveness of any muzzleloading big game rifle, more so if the rifle is loaded with a patched round ball.

• A scope makes sense when hunting the wide open spaces of the WEst. So does an extra-solid shooting rest such as the crossed sticks used here.

At 100 yards, the spheres of lead fired from .50- and .54-caliber muzzleloading hunting rifles have simply lost their "oomph"...upward of two-thirds the energy generated at the muzzle, to be exact. We've covered this in other chapters, but will give an example here again to stress the point.

A 90-grain charge of FFg black powder will push a patched round ball from the muzzle of a 24-inch barreled Knight rifle at about 1,750 fps. At this velocity, the 178-grain, .490-inch round ball generates in the neighborhood of 1,230 foot-pounds of energy. By the time the ball reaches 100 yards, it hits with less than 400 foot-pounds of energy -- hardly a potent big game load, even if the target is the relatively small pronghorn antelope. Most of today's frontloading rifles won't accurately handle a patched round ball when powder charges of more than 100 grains are loaded.

The 100-grain charge of Pyrodex "Select" Tom Fegely and I used on our Wyoming hunt pushes the saboted 260-grain pistol slug from the muzzle of a 24-inch barrel at about 1,525 fps. This is good for about 1,350 foot-pounds of energy. At 100 yards, the jacketed .45 bullet drives home with more than 1,000 foot-pounds of energy. Even if we load with just 90 grains of Pyrodex "Select", the bullet retains nearly 1,000 foot-pounds of energy at 100 yards. Now, which projectile do you think will do a better job at extended ranges?

This isn't to say that the round ball shooter should forget about hunting western game. Mule deer and antelope can be taken at closer ranges, it just takes different tactics. While settled in the ridge-top blind from where I took the trophy buck noted earlier in this chapter, I watched several fair bucks saunter past within 100 yards of where I was concealed. The round ball shooter could have taken those shots effectively. Similar blinds situated near hayfields and watering holes can also put the round ball shooter within effective range. These same tactics will work for mule deer just as well.

Hunting elk is more an experience than an exercise. An elk hunt is a trek into the back country, to get away from the hustle and bustle of everyday life. Since the special early muzzleloading elk seasons in several states allow a limited number of black powder hunters to experience a quality hunt at the peak of the bugling season, demand for the tags is at an all-time high...five or six hunters apply for every available tag.

From the smallest to the largest subspecies, elk are large, big bodied animals. A really big bull often weighs upward of a thousand pounds, and a few 1,500-pounders have been recorded. Most mature bulls will weigh between 600 and 800 pounds, while an adult cow will generally weigh upward of 400 pounds.

The muzzleloading hunter going after this big deer should rely on a rifle of large enough caliber and a load hefty enough to

Other Big Game

• *Gerry Blair with his black powder world record typical elk, taken in Arizona.*

do the job. In fact, in the half-dozen or so states with special muzzleloading hunts for elk, the smallest caliber allowed is the .50 caliber. If you plan to take one with a patched round ball, you might even consider the .54- or .58-caliber frontloader as the minimum.

When Lewis & Clark took their famous expedition across the plains and over the Rocky Mountains to the West Coast, the elk they encountered were dwellers of the plains and open country. Today's elk is an entirely different animal, in matters of habitat.

It's now rare to find a herd of elk lazily grazing out in the open, especially once opening morning of the centerfire season rolls around. In most regions of the West where elk are an important big game animal, modern rifle season opens in October or early November. At this time of year the rut is generally over and it's rare to hear a bull bugle. It's even rarer to lure one in close by bugling. The advantage of most early muzzleloader elk seasons is that they do take place when rut activity is at its highest.

While an experienced hunter who's good at calling can bugle a trophy bull to within 50 yards, the smart black powder burner will pack a rifle and load which will let him stretch that shot out to 100 to 150 yards, if and when necessary. This often means shooting loads that are right at maximum for the caliber and rifle model being carried.

This generally means relying on nothing less than a conical bullet, either of the bore diameter "maxi" type or a heavy saboted handgun bullet with 100- to 120-grain charges of FFg black powder or Pyrodex "RS" or "Select." Downing an elk with a muzzleloading rifle tests both the rifle and the hunter.

My favorite elk load for the .50-caliber rifle consists of 110 grains of Pyrodex "Select" behind a saboted .45-caliber jacketed soft-nose bullet. The load develops just over 1,600 fps muzzle velocity and nearly 1,500 foot-pounds of muzzle energy. At 100 yards it is still good for more than 1,150 foot-pounds of bone crunching energy, more than enough to down even a huge bull cleanly.

If I were to hunt a state or unit where saboted bullets are not allowed, my choice would be one of the 385 grain Hornady "Great Plains" bullets ahead of 110 grains of FFg black powder. Out of my rifle, this load is usually good for a three-inch group at 100 yards, not as good as the 1-3/4-inch groups I can shoot with the saboted .45 bullet but still plenty good for hunting elk. The big Hornady lead bullet leaves the muzzle at a slower 1,425 fps but generates a respectable 1,740 foot-pounds of muzzle energy. At a hundred yards it plows into its target with nearly 1,300 foot-pounds of energy.

Both Modern Muzzleloading and Muzzleload Magnum Products market a sabot which allows .54-caliber rifle owners to load and shoot the hard hitting pistol bullets for the big .50-caliber Desert Eagle handgun. One bullet I've been impressed with is the 325-grain Speer jacketed hollow-point in .50 caliber. While I haven't had an opportunity to shoot an elk with the bullet, I did use it to take a big aoudad ram at nearly a hundred yards. These are big wild sheep, weighing over 300 pounds. They are difficult to put down and keep down. Big bore centerfire shooters often have to put two or three shots into a ram before it stays put. Shooting 100 grains of Pyrodex "Select", one shot with the hefty hollow-point downed the big ram in his tracks.

My son Adam used the .50-caliber hollow point to take a beautiful ten-pointer on opening day of the Missouri whitetail season. He was shooting just 90 grains of Pyrodex "Select" in his .54-caliber rifle. His shot at 90 yards practically bowled the buck over in its tracks.

The first big game animal I witnessed being taken with the .50 caliber bullet out of a .54-caliber rifle was a record book central barren ground caribou taken by former Minnesota North Star hockey pro Steve Payne. He was shooting a television show and his cameraman captured the kill on tape, shooting right over Steve's shoulder as he made the 100-yard shot. The bull went about a hundred yards after being hit with a saboted, custom swaged, 350-grain, pure lead, hollow-point bullet made by Buckskin Bullet Company. Steve's shot was just a little back from where it should have been, but the bullet still did a great job and the bull went down within sight of the hunter.

On the same hunt I relied on the saboted 300-grain Speer jacketed soft nose and 110-grain powder charge prescribed earlier for elk to take a high-scoring record book bull at close to 200 yards. The big bullet caught the bull just behind the shoulder and angled through to exit just ahead of the opposite shoulder. The caribou went down in its tracks.

Glenn Thompson of North American Outdoor Adventures has the opportunity to

● *Outdoor writer Jim Shockey has so much faith in his in-line rifle it's the only gun he hunts with. He has taken everything from whitetails to a grizzly with a muzzleloader.*

Other Big Game

• *The author with a record-class central barren ground caribou, taken with a saboted 300 grain, .45 caliber pistol bullet at nearly 200 yards.*

hunt all over North America as he personally checks out many of the outfitters for which he books hunters. In recent years, Glenn has turned to muzzleloading as his preferred method of taking big game. In just the past couple years he has taken record book Quebec-Labrador, central barren ground, and woodland caribou with his .50-caliber rifle. He also shoots a 300-grain, .45-caliber, jacketed, soft-nose bullet but relies on 100 grains of FFg black powder. Glenn has used his muzzleloader on hunts for whitetails, desert bighorn sheep and moose as well.

Moose are tough to put down no matter what you're hunting them with. Just about any mature bull will top 1,000 pounds, and a few approaching 2,000 pounds are taken each season. When going after the biggest of this continent's deer, the key to success is a heavy powder charge and a bullet with enough weight to insure good penetration and high energy transfer.

My one and only muzzleloading moose was taken on an Alaskan hunt in 1989. I was hunting the upper Alaskan Peninsula about a hundred miles north of King Salmon. I'd spotted the bull practically from camp on the third day of the hunt. A 30 minute stalk put me about 75 yards from the 62-inch bull as it fed on aquatic grasses in a marshy depression.

It wasn't much of a shot. The rifle was a real tack driver and the big target stood broadside. The saboted 250-grain, .44-caliber, jacketed, Barnes hollow-point caught the bull squarely through the top of the heart and through both lungs.

At the shot, the animal showed little reaction to the hit. Instead, it cooperatively walked out of the knee deep water to higher ground, looked back in my direction and collapsed before I could get the rifle reloaded. I found the bullet under the hide of the opposite side.

On an earlier hunt with Garth Carter

• *A single saboted pistol bullet was all it took to cleanly take this big Alaska-Yukon moose.*

in almost the same area, I worked with Garth to get him a beautiful bull of the 60-inch class. Garth did it with a pipsqueak .45-caliber rifle.

For the hunt, Garth had worked up an 80-grain load of FFg behind a long 450-grain, soft lead conical bullet which had been cast in a custom cut mould. I was hesitant about the light powder charge, until he showed me that he could put the bullet exactly where it needed to go by dropping a nice barren ground caribou bull at about 150 yards just before the moose hunt.

After a successful three-day drop camp hunt for caribou, we flew north nearly a hundred miles for moose. From the air, we spotted a half dozen record-class bulls before finally locating a bull that was close enough to a lake for landing the float plane. Our pilot dropped us off about two miles from where we had seen two 60-inch bulls.

Alaska law prohibits hunting the same day that you're airborne. Since we couldn't hunt until the next morning, we spent the rest of the afternoon setting up camp and fishing for rainbow trout. Our pilot wouldn't return for six days, so we made camp as comfortable as possible.

Early the next morning, we were on a high ridge less than a mile from camp.

Working the ridge-top in the direction we had seen the two bulls the day before, it didn't take long to spot the wide, white palms of both bulls in the heavy growth between the ridge and the lake.

We both realized it would be extremely easy to get turned around in the thick stunted spruces between our ridge and the two bulls, so I decided to stay on the ridge-top and guide Garth's stalk from my vantage point. We both donned fluorescent orange caps to make spotting each other easy.

Every time Garth appeared in an opening below, I used hand signals to indicate the direction he needed to go. Nearly an hour later his bright orange cap appeared in the brush only a couple of hundred yards from the bulls, bedded now. Through the binoculars, I could see that he was asking for directions again. As soon as I knew he had me in his binoculars, I indicated that he needed to work back in the direction of the lake. Then, holding the palms of my hands close to each other, I tried to relay to him that he was getting close.

The message apparently got through. Garth slowly worked in the direction of the two bulls, his rifle ready. The distance separating them shortened to 150 yards, then 100 yards, and then 75 yards. It hadn't dawned on me that he still hadn't seen either of the bulls. He was less than 50 yards from the largest of the two when the bull stood up and Garth saw it for the first time.

I saw his rifle come to his shoulder, and a few seconds later a white puff of smoke appeared at the muzzle. In the same instant, the moose turned and ran, its wide white rack finally disappearing in the brush.

It took me 20 minutes to reach the spot where I thought I'd last spotted Garth. Just as I started to call out, I spotted a wide blood trail. Following it about a hundred yards, I broke through heavy undergrowth to find my partner sitting atop more than a thousand pounds of "Grade A Alaskan beef." One well-placed 450-grain slug had anchored the beautiful bull.

Garth had hoped to take an Alaska-Yukon bull which would meet the 180 Boone & Crockett point minimum for The Longhunter Society muzzleloading record book. The preliminary measurement of Garth's bull totaled nearly 220 points, which meant he had his record book bull with inches to spare.

A muzzleloader which will perform this well on elk, caribou and moose will perform well enough to warrant use on any North American big game animal, even the big bears. I've taken a number of black bears with a muzzleloader, including one big 502-pounder, and have found that hefty whitetail loads are all a hunter needs. For the bigger grizzly and coastal brown bears all I can say is to use something big and with plenty of punch. Even then don't take unnecessary chances; - have a good shot with a cool head back you with a powerful centerfire rifle or 12-gauge shotgun.

Going For The Record

Competition is a healthy and natural part of our daily lives. It's certainly good for business, forcing manufacturers to build the absolute best product they can and at a fair market price. If it wasn't for this sense of competition, the quality of the muzzleloading rifles we shoot and hunt with wouldn't be what it is today.

My son and I even share a little friendly competition when we head out for a morning or afternoon of bass fishing. It brings out the best in us. Whether you really care to admit it or not, there's also a competitive side to most of you reading this book. You know, that inner drive to out-shoot others during sighting in sessions, or to try to bring in a bigger buck than any of the other guys in camp.

Trophy hunting is a form of competition, even if it's with yourself. There's always that desire to take a bigger buck than you have in past seasons. If we didn't experience these feelings, most of us would be happy to tag the first legal whitetail that came along.

We now have a new record book for North American big game trophies taken with muzzleloader. It has done much to create a whole new breed of black powder shooter -- the serious trophy hunter who has taken up muzzleloading primarily to have a shot at getting an entry into the record books. The new Longhunter Society Big Game Record Book offers the black powder hunter that opportunity.

Bowhunters have had the Pope and Young record book for record-class North American big game animals, and the centerfire boys have had the prestigious Boone & crockett record book. (Note that any archery or muzzleloader trophy which scores high enough also qualifies for Boone & Crockett.) Of the three, the muzzleloading record book likely is the easiest to meet minimum qualifying scores.

Take a look at minimum qualifying scores for whitetail deer in all three books and you'll see what I mean.

To make the Pope and Young record book, a typical whitetail must score at least 125 points (B&C measurements). To qualify for the Boone & Crockett book, a typical whitetail must score a minimum of 170 B&C points. That's quite a difference. However, the Pope and Young book takes into consideration the degree of difficulty of getting within good range of even the most sophisticated bowhunting equipment.

Take a look at the minimum qualifying score – 130 B&C points – to place a typical whitetail buck in the Longhunter Society record book. That's right, just five points more than what it takes to get a typical whitetail into the Pope and Young record book. Even with the most primitive of reproduction rifles currently available, a good shooter can stretch his effective range out to 75 or 100 yards, easily twice to three times that of the average bowhunter.

Personally, I like the reasonable minimum qualifying scores. For most hunters, getting a whitetail buck or any other North American big game trophy into the Boone & Crockett record book is just a dream. With minimum qualifying scores which are only a few points higher than the Pope and Young archery record book, the Longhunter Society record book of muzzleloader-taken trophies is very reachable. Here are minimum entry scores for all North American big game species.

Species	Minimum Entry Score
Black Bear	18
Grizzly Bear	19
Alaska Brown Bear	21
Polar Bear*	22
Cougar (Mountain Lion)	13
American Elk (Wapiti) Typical	255
American Elk (Wapiti) Non-Typical	265
Roosevelt Elk (Wapiti)	225
Mule Deer (Typical)	146
Mule Deer (Non-Typical)	175
Columbia Blacktail Deer	95
Sitka Blacktail Deer	75
Whitetail Deer (Typical)	130
Whitetail Deer (Non-Typical)	160
Coues Whitetail Deer (Typical)	70
Coues Whitetail Deer (Non-Typical)	75
Canada Moose	145
Alaska-Yukon Moose	180
Wyoming (Shiras) Moose	125
Mountain Caribou	280
Woodland Caribou	230
Barren Ground Caribou	320
Central Canada Barren Ground Caribou	275
Quebec-Labrador Caribou	320
Pronghorn	63
Bison	92
Rocky Mountain Goat	41
Muskox	80
Bighorn Sheep	136
Desert Sheep	125
Dall's Sheep	132
Stone's Sheep	132

*Eligible only when taken and possessed in compliance with the Marine Mammals Act and other applicable regulations.

All scoring is done using the Boone & Crockett scoring system. **The Longhunter Society is the big game record keeping arm of the National Muzzle Loading Rifle Association, P.O. Box 67, Friendship, Indiana 47021.** For more information, write them.

Other Big Game

● *No matter where you go or what you do, take time to enjoy it all. Photo by Gary Clancy. There's more to the hunt than just the hunt.*

Chapter 14

The Future of Hunting With a Muzzleloader

By reading to this point you should be aware of how much the sport of muzzleloading has changed over the past couple of decades. Today's rifles are a far cry from longrifles carried across the Cumberland Gap by Daniel Boone, or which Davy Crockett took to Texas.

Muzzleloading has matured into a hunting sport, and today's black powder burner is a hunter. However, it would be virtually impossible for anyone to head for the deer woods with a muzzleloader thrown over his or her shoulder without some feeling for what it must have been like to hunt with a muzzleloader two hundred years ago, no matter how modern the frontloader being hunted with.

Still, there has been and remains a rift between the fanciers of traditionally-styled muzzleloading guns and those hunters who favor the better performance of percussion in-line ignition models. Many traditionalists feel there is no place for anything but a historically correct copy of the rifles carried by our forefathers. Others defend their choice of the in-line ignition system because of the better ballistics of modern projectiles and greater efficiency.

So, who is right? Should we allow only the traditionally styled muzzleloaders in order to save our heritage? Or should efficiency become the standard by which all hunting muzzleloaders are judged, eliminating those ignition systems and projectiles which simply can't stack up to defined efficiency and performance levels?

Those of us who also have bowhunted for a great number of years already have witnessed this scenario. In the late 1960s and early 1970s, when the compound bow was just appearing on the market, many traditional longbow and recurve bow shooters hated the new mechanical contraptions, claiming they were not bows at all and shouldn't be allowed during archery seasons. The hatred of the compound was so great that in many states legislation was proposed and occasionally passed to prohibit their use.

Fortunately, those days are behind us, those laws are repealed, and today's bowhunter is free to choose what he wants. Even so, the bowhunter who still wants the challenge and satisfaction of hunting with a non-mechanical bow has that right. Today, more than 90 percent of the archers who head afield do so carrying a compound bow, but the "traditional" archer may still cash in

• The selection of quality, well-built muzzleloading rifles is presently the best black powder shooters have ever had. Top photo — this is one of the Hatfield "Squirrel Rifles".

• Some of the modern in-line percussion rifles function so differently that even veteran black powder shooters need a little coaching the first time they pick one up. Photo above.

• Muzzleloading popularity has grown so much that it is now included in many state hunter education programs.

on the enjoyment of bowhunting his way.

When the first muzzleloading deer seasons were established, they were established as "opportunity seasons". The special seasons and hunts were to give an opportunity to experience what it was like to hunt with a design of firearm dating from the 1700s and 1800s.

Correspondingly, through the 1960s and on into the early 1970s, game departments were concerned about the overharvest of deer herds, which were just beginning to show signs of growth. In my home state of Illinois, when I first started hunting whitetails, it was difficult to get drawn for one of the coveted deer hunting permits. In many parts of the state there were three to four applications for every available permit.

The first year I hunted whitetails, Illinois boasted a deer herd of only 60,000 animals. Today, the state is home to more than 500,000 whitetails, and hunters can get up to four...five...six deer permits. Today, the concern in this state and in just about every other state where the whitetail is hunted is underharvest.

Muzzleloading today is playing an important management role in a growing number of states and more than likely will continue to grow in popularity. The reasons?

First, in most states the number of centerfire rifle and shotgun toting hunters during the general firearm deer seasons is already as great as most game departments would like. A few states, such as Michigan and Pennsylvania, will see around 1,000,000 deer hunters head for the woods come opening morning of the whitetail season. Think about that a minute. A million deer hunters all in the woods over the course of a week to two week deer season...in a single state. That's twice as many hunters looking to take a whitetail deer as we had troops in the Mid-East during all of "Operation Desert Storm".

While whitetail herds continue to grow, game departments continue to look for new ways to manage the ever-expanding resource. Few opt to lengthen the modern firearm season, feeling that they are already trying to control as many hunters afield for as long a period as they like. These same game departments have already made archery seasons just about as liberal as they can, providing up to three months to hunt and liberal limits.

Muzzleloading seasons, many still relatively new in a number of states, are giving game departments another management tool to better control the growing whitetail populations.

One thing is for certain, and that is that muzzleloading hunters enjoy a much higher success rate than bowhunters. Archers rarely jump above the 10 percent success rate, or in other words rarely will 100,000 bowhunters tag 10,000 deer during the course of a season. Bowhunting still is not a serious herd management tool in some states, but it is in others.

Black powder hunters tend to enjoy fairly high success rates. I have been on controlled area hunts where the success rate ran as high as 90 percent, but on some of them only a hundred to two hundred permits may have been issued. Even so, in most statewide muzzleloading hunts, the muzzleloading hunter often enjoys a 30 percent to 40 percent success rate. In a state which may issue 50,000 muzzleloading permits, the harvest can account for 15,000 to 20,000 whitetails, which can represent a significant percentage of a state's overall whitetail harvest and be a serious management tool.

The black powder hunter isn't faced with quite as limited a range as the bowhunter; for the average shooter it's much easier to learn to hit a deer-sized target at 50 or 75 yards with a muzzleloader than it is to put an arrow where it needs to go at 20 yards. This, coupled with the fact that most muzzleloading hunters are a lot happier about harvesting a doe than are a large percentage of modern firearm hunters, allows game departments to manage the doe population.

Muzzleloader hunting continues to be the happy middle ground, bringing converts from both bowhunting and modern firearm hunting. We have the bowhunter who just isn't comfortable with taking up hunting deer or other big game with a centerfire rifle or, where required, a shotgun and slugs. However, he will move over into muzzleloading

• *Teenager Carl Renfrow with his first muzzleloading whitetail. Hunting with a muzzleloader is attracting hunters of all ages and from all walks of life.*

to cash in on the bonus hunting provided by a second season. On the other side are those modern gun hunters who have no intention of trying to take a deer with a bow, but, like the bowhunter, will move into muzzleloading for the same bonus hunting opportunities.

Many of the states which began with a short three- or five-day muzzleloading season offer today two or more muzzleloader seasons or one that has been lengthened considerably. Every state now offers either a muzzleloader-only season or, at the very least, special muzzleloading hunts on wildlife management areas.

It was the establishment of muzzleloading seasons which can be credited with bringing the largest number of shooters and hunters to muzzleloading. It was the lure of hunting a "third season" and the bonus hunting time afield, and the opportunity to tag additional game in some states, which caused many shooters to pick up a muzzleloader for the first time. Like the bowhunter who now readily accepts the technology of the compound bow, today's muzzleloading hunter is looking to hunt with the most efficient equipment and loads available.

It's unfortunate that hard core traditionalists feel threatened by the advanced technology of today's hunting muz-zleloaders. They shouldn't. (Besides, most of the "reproduction" rifles presently available are a far cry from being true copies of the guns made 150 to 200 years ago.) Muzzleloading fans come in a wide range of equipment preferences, and there's room for all.

We have gained the majority of "muzzleloader only" hunting time we currently enjoy simply because the sport now appeals to a much broader spectrum of hunters than if the special season allowed only truly traditional muzzleloading designs. The safety, accuracy and reliability of today's more modern muzzleloading rifles have undoubtedly brought new people into muzzleloading.

What's happening with muzzleloading today is an exact parallel with what happened in bowhunting. Once archers stopped fussing and fighting among themselves over what was a bow and what wasn't, and started working together for the betterment of bowhunting, their hunting opportunities skyrocketed. The same will happen with muzzleloading.

As human populations grow even more dense in many regions of the country, we're sure to see increasing restrictions on the use of flat-shooting, long-range centerfire rifles. It's inevitable that we'll see more "shotgun only" restrictions for hunting whitetails, and in every instance the muzzleloading rifle will likely be offered as an option for those hunters who demand better accuracy than a hunter can get with a shotgun and slugs. The limited range of a frontloading rifle, coupled with the single-shot capacity of most models, make muzzleloaders ideal for use in more-populated areas.

Muzzleloading has a bright future, but only if today's black powder shooter will give it the opportunity to grow. No longer can we divide into special interest niches and feud among ourselves. The only way we'll expand muzzleloading hunting opportunities is by forgetting our differences in hardware preferences and working together.

The Publisher

Target Communications publishes hunting, archery and wild game cooking books and produces deer / turkey hunting consumer expositions and shooting sports shows.

This book is the company's twelfth title. A complete list of their current titles is given on page 148.

The six expositions and shooting sports shows which the company produces are:
- Wisconsin Deer & Turkey Expo & Shooting Sports Show, Madison;
- Michigan Deer & Turkey Spectacular & Shooting Sports Show, Lansing;
- Illinois Deer & Turkey Classic & Shooting Sports Show, Peoria;
- Ohio Deer & Turkey Expo & Shooting Sports Show, Columbus;
- Pennsylvania Deer & Turkey Expo & Shooting Sports Show, King of Prussia;
- Volunteer State (TN) Hunting Classic & Shooting Sports Show, Nashville.

Target Communications president, Glenn Helgeland, has been a deer hunter all his hunting life, with rifle and bow. He edited *Archery World,* now *Bowhunting World,* magazine 11 years (1970-1980), and won awards from the National Archery Association (NAA) for service to archery and from the National Shooting Sports Foundation (NSSF) for a series of articles titled "The Hunter's Story".

He has been, at various times, bowhunting columnist for *American Hunter, North American Hunter* and *Bowhunting World.*

Helgeland co-authored with John Williams, 1972 Olympic archery gold medalist, the book "Archery For Beginners". He also edited the Second Edition of the Pope and Young Club's Big Game Records Book.

He was named, in 1985, as one of the "50 Who Made A Difference" to the sport of archery / bowhunting by the publishers of *Archery Business* magazine.

Helgeland also has been an associate editor of *National Wildlife* magazine.

The "On Target" Series

UNDERSTANDING WINNING ARCHERY, by Al Henderson, coach of the 1976 U.S. Olympic Archery Team, international coach and shooting consultant. Mental control means easier archery gear set-up, more-productive practices and winning archery. Book #01-001.

TAKING TROPHY WHITETAILS (2nd Edition), by Bob Fratzke with Glenn Helgeland. In-depth, detailed information, well illustrated, on year-round scouting, scrape hunting, rut hunting, late season hunting, camouflage, use of scents, plus entire new chapter on mock scraping and licking branches. Book #01-003.

SUCCESSFUL BOWFISHING, by Glenn Helgeland. A coast-to-coast, in-depth view of an enjoyable extension of your bowhunting. Freshwater and saltwater, carp to sharks, plus gear set-up, boat and canoe rigging, light diffraction and more. Book #01-004.

TO HECK WITH GRAVY wild game cookbook, by Glenn and Judy Helgeland. Gourmet results from 209 quick, easy recipes. Plus meat handling/processing tips, seasonings chart, low-sodium diet tips and more. Book #01-005.

TASTY JERKY RECIPES FOR EVERYONE, by Glenn and Judy Helgeland. Spicy, mild, sweet and no-sodium recipes for three different meat cut thicknesses and tendernesses. Make in oven, smoker, dehydrator or microwave. Book #01-006.

TUNING YOUR COMPOUND BOW (2nd Edition), by Larry Wise, the recognized master of understanding and interpreting the mechanics of compound bows. Includes pre-use bow preparation, draw stroke, power stroke, shooting from the valley, fine tuning, test shooting, plus tuning the Fast Flite cable system, building and tuning aluminum and carbon arrows. Book #01-008.

TUNING YOUR BROADHEADS & Entire Bowhunting System (2nd Edition), by Larry Wise. Problem-solving information on fitting the bow to your body and shooting form; broadhead effects on arrow flight; noise reduction; aiming and shooting strategies; proper practice; plus tuning the Fast Flite cable system, building and tuning aluminum and carbon arrows. Book #01-009.

TUNING & SHOOTING YOUR 3-D BOW, by Larry Wise. Explains the 3-D archery game and who shoots it; arrow speed - the 3-D advantage; 3-D archery and bowhunting. Detailed information on choosing the right equipment, the force-draw curve of a cam, choosing and tuning 3-D arrows, shooting your 3-D bow, practice strategies for 3-D and for bowhunting, and shooting 3-D competition. Book #01-010.

BECOME THE ARROW (the Art of Modern Barebow Shooting), by Byron Ferguson with Glenn Helgeland. Details the "become the arrow" philosophy; walks you step-by-step through that shooting system; explains how to visualize arrow flight path and sight picture; shooting form practice and mental exercises; how to develop the necessary focus and concentration; tuning for barebow shooting; bowhunting details on moon phases and other advanced items; most-commonly asked questions, building a longbow. Book #01-011.

MUZZLELOADING FOR WHITETAILS & Other Big Game, by Toby Bridges, the nation's foremost black powder hunter/writer. Black powder technology, and rifles, have changed dramatically the past ten years with the introduction of the percussion in-line style. More and better black powder hunting seasons now are the big draw; traditionalism is waning. Here's the most up-to-date technical data on black powder rifles (new and traditional) and accessories, plus detailed, no-nonsense tips on the special knowledge needed to make your black powder hunting more productive. Book #01-012.

See your dealer or order direct from the publisher.

Write or call for a free catalog:
TARGET COMMUNICATIONS CORPORATION
7626 W. Donges Bay Rd.
Mequon, WI 53097
414-242-3990   1-800-324-3337